COMFORT FOOD

Enjoy Everyday With Homemade Comfort Food and Stew
Cookbook

(Delicious Recipes for Real Comfort Food)

Robert Mills

Published by Alex Howard

Comfort Food: Enjoy Everyday With Homemade Comfort Food and Stew Cookbook (Delicious Recipes for Real Comfort Food)

ISBN 978-1-990169-59-5

Legal & Disclaimer

The information contained in this book is not designed to replace or take the place of any form of medicine or professional medical advice. The information in this book has been provided for educational and entertainment purposes only.

Table of contents

Part 1

Chapter 1: Spiralizer Tools and Techniques

With new and interesting twists and variations in cooking, spiralizer is a tool that can make you love cooking and eating your veggies. There are many different types of spiralizers out there. Besides the types, you should also know the best brands when you want to buy one. Turn your veggies into thin strings with a spiralizer and use your creativity to make the best dishes!

Types of Spiralizers

Mainly there are three types of spiralizers:

Hand Held Spiralizers

It is the cheapest option but requires some hard work. It takes vegetables of size 2"/5cm or even less.

Horizontal Hold Spiralizers

These spiralizers can easily manage much larger vegetables than the hand held ones. They hold the vegetables in place with a small metal ring. It is a bit wasteful as well because it cuts the core the size of a pencil. So, it's not very good for thinner vegetables. Besides that, the vegetables slip out of place even with the metal ring.

Vertical Hold Spiralizers

Vertical spiralizers are the best option because the vegetables don't slip out of place and they work faster than the other two options. The vegetable sits on top of the blade and the pressure is exerted downwards as you turn the handle. You get the nice long and thin strings of vegetables very quickly. A spike holds the vegetable in place and it also does not waste any part of the veggies. But it takes smaller and thinner vegetables. So, you have to cut vegetables before putting them on the vertical spiralizer.

Best Spiralizers in the Market

While buying a spiralizer, you should look for 5 things:

1. Ease of use
2. Easy to clean
3. Strength and durability
Size
Additional features like different types of blades that are easy to fix and remove.

Lurch Super Spiralizer

The quality that makes this German brand Lurch one of the best spiralizers is the ease of use. It has the easiest handle function which requires very less pressure to put in the fruits and vegetables through the blade. The spike pad has a very good grip. The suction feet prevent it from shaking while you are using it. It also offers three attachments that are stored in the drawers made in the foot of the spiralizer. The ribbons come out perfectly nice and long.

Benriner Cook Helper Slicer

This Japanese spiralizer is best for hard vegetables. It has a vertical orientation which makes it easy to apply enough pressure to make nice and thin ribbons. It is lightweight and smaller than the horizontal spiralizers which make it easy to tuck it in a cupboard. The blades are very sharp. It is a brilliant piece of machinery which works perfectly.

Paderno World Cuisine Spiralizer Pro

Its features are very good:

- 4 blades
- BPA free
- 1 year warranty
  Dishwasher safe
- Under $50

Besides these basic features, it comes with a folding body which makes it easy to store. You can use any kind of fruits and vegetables to make fun pasta dishes.

iPerfect Kitchen Vegetable Spiralizer Bundle

A handy and compact tool, this spiralizer can bring an awesome twist to your pasta dishes. Its key features can blow you away:

- Easy to use like a pencil sharpener
- Dishwasher safe
  Durable
- BPA free
- Easy to store
- Not expensive – under $15
- Includes helpful e-books about recipes, cleaning instruction and more

Tips and Techniques on Using a Spiralizer

Using a spiralizer is not rocket science. Once you figure it out, you can make yummy fruit and veggie noodles any time you want. Most of them come with three different blades:

1. A Thinner Noodle: It resembles the thickness of spaghetti. Use it to make Italian or Asian noodles.
2. A Thinner Ribbon: This blade gives you a beautiful and thin ribbon spiral. Use it to make salads or almost anything you want.
3. A Thicker Spiral: This spiral can also be used in a variety of dishes. You can also make curly fries from different vegetables. Be as creative as you can be!

Once you have selected a blade of your choice, choose a vegetable and stick it on the spike pad or a holding ring, according to your machine. Then start turning the handle and you get nice noodles or ribbons. If you are using a cheaper hand-held spiralizer, you have to use it like a pencil sharpener. You can also consult the instructions manual that comes with the spiralizer.

Which Vegetables are the Best?

Let's jump to the fun part: which vegetables to use and what to make of them? There are so many options for you that you will really love using your spiralizer. Here are a few quick ideas:

- Use a thinner noodle blade to make Italian pasta dishes from potatoes, parsnips, rutabagas, sweet potatoes, turnips, kohlrabi, and zucchini.
- For Asian stir-fry or soup noodles, again use a thinner noodle blade. The best vegetables for this purpose are: potatoes, carrots, zucchini, turnips, and radishes.
- Make 'courgetti' instead of spaghetti to cut back on carbs. Use a thinner noodle blade and boil courgette for 20 seconds. Sauce or toppings is your choice.
- Carrots ribbons are perfect for making salads. You can also stir-fry them with garlic and coconut oil.
- Apples and mooli make a nice and crunchy salad. Just make sure to use lemon juice on apples to stop them from turning brown.
- Make Pad Thai using bell peppers or zucchini. While zucchini is easier to spiralize, bell peppers are tricky. Cut off the head and place the other end on the blade and spiral away.
- Use the flat blade to spiralize cabbage and onions as they are already in layers.
- Yellow squash is the prettiest and easiest to spiralize just like zucchini. Add it in dish you like.

Whether you make pasta, salads, stir-fry the vegetables, make soup, bake, or make fries; the texture and taste of these vegetables will be great. The best thing about a spiralizer is that it's healthy for you. You get to eat loads of vegetables in a fun way without noticing that these are the same boring veggies many of us didn't really want to eat before spiralizing them. You can control your weight by adding more veggies in your diet. Besides weight control, eating vegetables and fruits improves your stomach, skin, and overall health because it increase your intake of fiber, minerals, and vitamins that you miss out when you are eating fewer vegetables. So, make healthy changes in your lifestyle by cooking delicious and easy vegetarian meals.

Chapter 2: vegetarian spiralizer pasta recipes

Pasta is one of the most favorite dishes of people all over the world due to an abundance of flavor, variety and health benefits it offers. And if you use a spiralizer to chop down vegetables and fruits for your pasta, you won't be able to resist devouring it till the last bite. The most exciting thing about using a spiralizer while making pasta is that you can use it to transform the simplest of ingredients into a gorgeous mouthwatering dish. Here are a few yummy vegetarian spiralizer pasta recipes:

Celeriac Pasta Recipe with Apple and Walnut Sauce

The delightful combination of spiralized celeriac along with lime juice and the beautiful apple and walnut sauce is what makes it a mind-blowing recipe. It's the perfect treat for children on weekends and holidays.

Ingredients for Pasta:

1. ½ Celeriac Cabbage
2. 1 chopped Green onion
3. Lime juice – 3 tbsp
4. Sesame seeds, sunflower seeds, fresh thyme and/or pumpkin for topping

Ingredients for the Sauce:

1.1 Apple – peeled and diced
2. Raw Mustard – ½ tsp
3. Black Pepper
4. Walnut oil – 3 tbsp
5. Lime juice – 1 tbsp
6. Honey – 1 tsp

Method:

- Peel the celeriac and use a spiralizer to make pasta. Add lime juice to your pasta and put it aside.
- Take a blender and toss in all the ingredients for the sauce. Blend until smooth.
- In a bowl, add the pasta and pour the sauce on it. Refrigerate it for a day and then enjoy this scrumptious dish!

Carrot Pasta with Lemon, Ginger and Peanut Sauce

Carrot pasta is a simple but exceedingly delicious and healthy pasta recipe that makes use of basic ingredients like raw carrots, cashews, peanut butter, ginger, and lemon juice, etc.

Ingredients for Pasta:

1.5 Large peeled carrots, spiraled into noodles
2. Finely sliced fresh cilantro – 2 tbsp
3. Roasted cashews – 1/3 cup

Ingredients for the Sauce:

1. Liquid amino and peanut butter (creamy) – 2 tbsp each
2. Coconut milk – 4 tbsp
3. A pinch of cayenne pepper
4. 2 Peeled and diced garlic cloves
5. Peeled and diced fresh ginger – 1 tbsp
6. 1 tbsp lemon juice

Method:

•Wash the carrots, peel them and let them dry. Make carrot noodles using a spiralizer.

Take a bowl and add all the sauce ingredients in it. Stir until you get a creamy and smooth mix.

• Put you carrot noodles in another bowl. Then pour the sauce on the noodles and mix gently.

•Decorate it with roasted cashews and fresh cilantro and serve!

Carrot Pasta with Garlic Sauce

Ever thought of raw pasta? If no, then here is a delicious, light and a healthy version of typical Italian pasta. The carrot pasta is crunchy and fresh which is combined exquisitely with a creamy and zesty garlic sauce.

Ingredients:

1. 1 spiralized carrot
2. Tahini – 1 tbsp
3. Fresh lime juice – 3 tbsp
4. 1 small grated garlic clove
5. Olive oil – 1 tbsp
6. Grated ginger – 1 tsp
7. Tamari – 1 tsp
8. Pine nuts, sesame seeds and parsley for topping

Method:
- Mix all the ingredients to make the sauce, except the pasta and the toppings.
- Pour the sauce over the carrots and toss well.
- Then sprinkle the toppings and keep it in the fridge overnight.

It seems more like a salad but you can always enjoy this raw pasta whenever you want. It is just fantastic.

Zucchini Noodle and Ginger Scallion Recipe

If you are a fan of spicy food, then you must try this delectable recipe. The epic flavor of this dish originates from the blend of zucchini, scallions, red pepper and ginger.

Ingredients:

1. 1 medium-sized zucchini – spiralized into noodles
2. Virgin olive oil – ¾ tbsp
3. Chopped scallions – ½ cup
4. Dried seaweed – 3 tbsp
5. Soy sauce(low-sodium) – 1 tbsp
6. Sherry vinegar – 2 tsp
7. 16oz Vegetable Broth
8. ½ cup water
9. Grated ginger – 1 tbsp
10. Black pepper and Red pepper flakes, to taste

Method:

• Heat olive oil in a large pan at medium heat. Add ginger and cook it for a minute.
• Add soy sauce, sherry vinegar, vegetable broth, pepper flakes and water and let it cook till it boils.
• Then add seaweed and slowly whisk in the egg. Put in the scallions, zucchini noodles and pepper and cook the mixture

for 2 minutes.
- Place it in a serving bowl and enjoy while it's hot.

Pear Noodles with Fruit Cocktail and Yogurt

This fresh and yummy pasta dessert is something your kids will fall in love with. The freshness of fruits and yogurt together with pear noodles will make them demand this dish every now and then.

Ingredients:

1. Diced bananas, strawberries or blueberries - 1/3 cup
2. Greek Yogurt (flavored or unflavored)
3. 1/3 cup of your favorite granola
4. Pear noodles of 2 medium sized pears

Method:

• Take a mason jar and add the fruit in it. Then add 1 container of yogurt.
• Top the yogurt with granola and add pear noodles at the end.
• Put a spoon in the jar and enjoy!

Broccoli Noodle Pasta with Garlic Roasted Pine Nuts

Broccoli noodle pasta is a fusion of flavorful ingredients and simple cooking techniques. It's an easy-to-make recipe that contains an abundance of nutrients and vitamins in it.

Ingredients:

1. 1 Broccoli head together with its stem
2. Olive oil – 2 tbsp
3. Red pepper flakes – 1 pinch
4. Pecorino romano cheese, lime juice, pine nuts – 1 tbsp each
5. 3 Finely sliced garlic cloves
6. Salt and pepper (to taste)

Method:

• Cut off the broccoli head, leaving on the florets as little stem as possible. Put the florets aside. Cut the bottom side of the stem to make it evenly flat. Use your spiralizer to make noodles from the stem.
• Take a large skillet and heat olive oil in it at medium heat. Add broccoli florets, noodles, pepper flakes, salt and pepper. Cover

it and cook the mixture for 3 to 5 minutes while frequently shaking the skillet.

• In the meantime, take another pan and roast the pine nuts in it for 5 minutes at medium heat. Once done, put the nuts aside.

• Whisk in the lime juice and garlic and cook the broccoli noodle mix for another 3 to 5 minutes. Keep it covered. When it's done, place it in a serving bowl and top it with pine nuts and romano cheese.

Potato Pasta Delight with Toasted Garlic Parmesan

A single bite of potato noodle pasta with toasted garlic parmesan will be an unforgettable treat for your taste buds. The smoothness of the noodles and the subtle flavor of parmesan cheese and garlic makes it a heavenly delight.

Ingredients:

1.2 lbs. of red potatoes. Use your Spiralizer to make noodles
2. Virgin olive oil (extra) – 1 tbsp
3. Garlic powder – ½ tsp
4. Salt and pepper to taste
5.Minced parsley – 2 tbsp

Method:

• Preheat your oven to 425°F. Put the potato noodles in a bowl and whisk in the olive oil. Lay out the noodles on a baking sheet (parchment-paper lined). Use salt and pepper for seasoning. Then add garlic and roast it in the oven for 12 to 15 minutes or until golden brown.
• Take out the noodles and set the mixture to broil. Sprinkle

parmesan cheese and bake it for another 3 to 5 minutes.
- Remove the noodles from the oven and sprinkle parsley to decorate. Serve while the pasta is hot.

Butternut Squash Noodle Pasta with Brussels sprouts, Caramelized Onions and Walnuts

Normally brussels sprouts aren't very famous among people, especially kids but this amazing recipe will make them rethink their opinion about this healthy vegetable.

Ingredients:

1. 1 medium-sized peeled and spiralized butternut squash
2. Extra virgin olive – 2½ tbsp
3. Garlic powder – ¼ tsp
4. Salt and pepper, as per your taste
5. Chopped walnut – ½ cup
6. Brussels Sprouts – 1 cup
7. 1 pulverized garlic clove
8. Red pepper flakes – ¼ tsp
9. Crumbled parmesan cheese – ¼ cup (optional)

Method:

• Preheat your oven to 400°F. Take a baking sheet and lay out the noodles, drizzle ¼ teaspoon of olive oil and season with salt pepper and garlic powder. Prepare another tray and line it with parchment paper. Put the walnut in that tray. Bake the noodles for about 10 minutes and the walnuts for about 5 minutes.
• In the meantime, shave the brussels sprouts by chop of the bottom, cutting them in half and finely slicing them (lengthwise).
• Take a large skillet and heat the remaining olive oil at medium heat. Once heated, add onion, pulverized garlic and pepper flakes and cook the mix on medium-low heat for about 3 minutes.
• Put in the brussels sprouts and add some salt and pepper for seasoning. Keep it on low-heat, cover with a lid and cook for

about 3 to 5 minutes while stirring occasionally. Then take the lid off and add walnuts and parmesan cheese and stir properly.
• Take a serving bowl and toss in the mixture along with butternut squash noodles and mix well. Serve it hot!

Thread Noodles with Courgettes and Green Papaya

Composed of flavorful ingredients and tons of healthy nutrients, this is a "must try" recipe for any vegetarian who wishes to be dazzled.

Ingredients:
1. Thread noodles – ½ cup
2. 1 Peeled and spiralized green papaya (deseeded)
3. Lightly roasted cashew nuts – ½ cup
4. 1 finely chopped red chilli
5. Sea Salt (to taste)
6. A small peeled and chopped ginger
7. Groundnut oil – 3 tbsp
8. Soy sauce, lime juice and palm sugar – 1 tbsp each
9. Coriander and mint leaves

Method:

• Take bowl, add hot and salted water in it and soak the noodles for about 15 minutes. Then take the noodles out, drain well and set aside.

- In a mixing bowl, mix cashews, papaya, courgette and noodles. Prepare the dressing by blending sugar, soy sauce, garlic, chilli and ginger. Whisk in the oil and lime juice and combine the mixture with noodles, courgette and papaya.
- Garnish it with coriander and mint leaves and enjoy this scrumptious dish!

Zucchini Pasta with Parmesan Cheese and Toasted Artichokes

Zucchini is used in numerous recipes, but in this particular recipe the use of zucchini along with roasted artichokes, lime juice and parmesan will light up your mood and you wouldn't want to stop eating this yummy dish.

Ingredients:

1. A can of halved artichokes, drained and dried
2. Extra virgin olive oil – 2 tbsp
3. Garlic powder – ½ tsp
4. 3 zucchinis
5. 2 pressed garlic cloves
6. Salt and pepper (to taste)
7. Red pepper flakes – ¼ tsp
8. Lime juice – 1 tbsp
9. Crumbled parmesan cheese – ¼ cup

Method:

• Preheat your oven to 425°F. Take a mixing bowl and add in the garlic powder, artichokes, salt, pepper and 1 tablespoon olive oil. Mix well and spread out the artichokes on a parchment paper lined baking sheet. Bake the artichokes for about 20 minutes (or until brown).

- In the meantime, spiralize the zucchini and put it aside.
- After 10 minutes of baking the artichokes, take a large skillet and heat 1 tablespoon of olive oil at medium heat. Add pepper flakes and garlic in heated oil and cook until fragrant. Then add zucchini noodles, salt and pepper and cook for about 5 minutes while stirring.
- After that add in the lime juice, roasted artichokes and parmesan. Remove the mix from heat and stir well.
- Transfer it in a serving bowl and serve.

Chapter 3: spiralizer stir fry recipes

Stir Fry Zucchini Noodles

Stir Fry Zucchini Noodles are delicious and low carb. They are made with spiralized zucchini and onions which are nicely tossed in teriyaki sauce and toasted sesame seeds.

Ingredients:

1. 4 spiralized medium sized zucchinis - dried with towels
2. 2 spiralized medium sized yellow onions
3. Teriyaki sauce – 2 tbsp
4. Sesame seeds – 1 tbsp
5. Soy sauce – 1 tbsp
6. Vegetable oil – 2 tbsp

Method:

• Heat oil in a wok or a frying pan over medium heat
• Add onions and cook for 5 minutes.
  Toss in the zucchini and cook for 2 minutes.
• Add teriyaki sauce, sesame seeds, and soy sauce. Keep on tossing the noodles for 5 minutes.
• Remove from heat and serve immediately.

It is so simple that you can make it any time. Plus, it tastes awesome.

Stir Fry Sweet Potato and Zucchini Noodles

Stir fried veggie noodles make a great combination with different sauces. This recipe also offers delicacy of taste in simplicity. Go ahead and try it!

Ingredients:
For Noodles:

1.1 spiralized large sized sweet potato
2. 1 spiralized medium sized zucchini
3. Olive oil – 1 tbsp
4. Minced garlic – 1 tbsp

For sauce:

1. Soy sauce – 3 tbsp
2. Honey 1 tsp
3. Corn starch – 1 tsp
4. Sesame oil – 1 tsp
5.Hoison sauce – 1 tbsp
6.Brown sugar – ½ tbsp
7. Freshly minced ginger root – 1 tsp
8.Sriracha sauce(optional)

Method:

• Heat olive oil in a large frying pan over high heat and stir fry garlic for 1 minute.
• Toss in the sweet potatoes and cook for 2 minutes.
• Then stir fry the zucchini for 1 minute.
• Combine the sauce ingredients in a bowl and pour it over the noodles. Cook the noodles until they are a little tender but not too soft.

That's it! They are ready to be devoured.

Butternut Squash Spaghetti

Combine the sweetness and warmth of spiralized butternut squash with the creamy ricotta and green leafy vegetables to enjoy a healthier version of the Italian pasta recipe.

Ingredients:

1.1 butternut squash – peeled and halved
2. Ricotta cheese – ½ cup
3. Juice of one lemon
4. 1 crushed garlic clove
5. Frozen peas – ½ cup
6.Baby spinach – ½ cup
7. Sunflower oil – 1 tbsp
8. Freshly ground black pepper and salt – to taste
9. Freshly grated parmesan cheese – for topping

Method:

- Spiralize the squash.
- Take a small bowl and mix the herbs, lemon juice and ricotta.
- Heat oil in a large skillet over medium heat. Stir fry garlic for

one minute. Then toss in the squash and cook for 5 minutes. Then add peas and spinach and cook for 2 minutes.

• Add the sauce and 4 tbsp of boiling water. Stir well for 2 minutes to coat the sauce properly. Season with salt and pepper and sprinkle some parmesan cheese.

Serve immediately and enjoy the flavors of this beautiful dish.

Korean BBQ Zoodle

Spiralizers have brought an interesting twist in carb-rich Asian recipes, including this Korean BBQ Zoodle. Use spiralized vegetables instead of regular noodles and you will know how fantastic they are!

Ingredients:

1. 3 spiralized zucchinis
2. Broccoli florets – 2 cups
3. Halved Brussels sprouts – 2 cups
4. Spiralized purple cabbage and carrots – 2 cups
5. Diced onion – ¼ cup
6. 2 diced spring onions
7. 2 minced garlic cloves
8. 8 white button mushrooms (quartered)
9. Coconut oil – 1 tbsp
10. Thinly sliced quarter avocado
11. Korean BBQ sauce – half cup
12. Salt and pepper – to taste
13. Sesame seeds and hot sauce – for topping

Method:

• Sauté garlic and onions in a large frying pan over medium heat.

- Add Brussels sprouts and cook for 6 minutes.
- Add the rest of the vegetables, except zucchini noodles and cook for 5 minutes.
- Now mix the sauce and put away from heat. Let it rest while you evenly divide the zoodles in the bowls. Then add the sauce, sprinkle some avocados and sesame seeds, and finally a little hot sauce equally in all the bowls.

No one will ever refuse these mouth-watering Korean zoodles!

Stir Fry Rainbow Noodles

These noodles are colorful and very delicious. It is a fun way to serve veggies to those who are not really big fans of eating their vegetables.

Ingredients:

1. 1 spiralized carrot
2. 1 spiralized zucchini
3. 1 spiralized red bell pepper
4. Spiralized purple cabbage – ½ cup
5. Chopped collard greens – 1/2 cup
6. 1 spiralized onion
7. Chopped ginger – 1 tbsp
8. Chopped garlic – 1 tbsp
9. Chopped Swiss chard – half cup
10. Sesame oil – 1 tbsp
11. Cumin – 1 tbsp
12. Lemon juice – 1 tbsp
13. Cayenne – half tsp
14. Salt – to taste
15. Sesame seeds for garnish

Method:

- Boil zucchini and carrot noodles for 2 minutes. Drain and set aside.
- Heat oil in a large frying pan over medium heat. Sauté ginger, garlic and onions for 2 minutes. Add the remaining ingredients except the boiled noodles and cook for 5-7 minutes. Turn off the stove, add the noodles and mix well.

Garnish with sesame seeds and enjoy!

Stir Fry Veggie Noodles

Vegetables look so different and tasty when you spiralize them. This is what this recipe is all about. It combines all the harmonious flavors to ignite your hunger.

Ingredients:

1. 3 spiralized zucchinis
2. 1 spiralized red bell pepper
3. 2 spiralized carrots
4. 5 diced green onions
5. Broccoli florets – 2 cups
6. Snap peas – ¾ cup
7. 3 small heads of chopped Bok Choy (separate the stems and leaves)
8. Sliced mushrooms – 1 cup
9. Freshly grated ginger – half tsp
10. 2 finely minced garlic cloves
11. Olive oil – 2 tbsp
12. Soy sauce – 2 tbsp
13. Salt and pepper – to taste

Method:

- Heat a large frying pan over medium heat. Then add oil, garlic, and green onions and cook for 1 minute.
- Then add Bok Choy stems and peas and cook for 2 minutes. After that, toss in the mushrooms, broccoli, and Bok Choy leaves. Sauté for 2 minutes.
- Add the spiralized zucchini, bell pepper and carrot. Throw in 2 tablespoons of soy sauce, cover the pan and let it cook for 2 minutes.
- Remove the cover, sprinkle the ginger and season with salt and pepper.

Toss it thoroughly and enjoy the yummy stir fried veggie noodles.

Zucchini Noodles with Cashews

Zoodles taste heavenly with nuts, especially if the zoodles are dressed with appetizing sauce and topped with cashew nuts. Go for it and you will know how amazing it is!

Ingredients:
For the Sauce:

1. Hoison sauce – 1 tbsp
2. Dark soy sauce – ¼ cup
3. Arrow root powder – 2 tbsp
4. Sriracha sauce – 1 tsp
5. Sesame oil – half tsp
6. Brown sugar – half tsp
7. Rice vinegar – 1 tsp

For the rest of the dish:

1. 4 spiralized carrots
2. 2 spiralized and zucchini (dry off the excess liquid)
3. 2 spiralized red bell peppers
4. Snow peas – 1 ¼ cups
5. 2 finely minced garlic cloves
6. Half yellow onion, diced
7. Roughly chopped cashews – 1 cup

Method:

- Mix the ingredients of the sauce in a small bowl.
- Heat oil in a large skillet over high heat. Add garlic and onion. Sauté until they are fragrant and toss in the spiralized vegetables and snap peas. Toss them thoroughly and turn down the heat. Gently add the sauce and let it thicken for 5 minutes. Add 2/3 cashews and mix well.
- Put it in the bowls and sprinkle the remaining cashews over the top.

You would just love to eat it and want more and more!

Sautéed Zoodle Ribbons

This recipe is not simply about zucchini ribbons. It brings together sun dried tomatoes, artichoke hearts, kalamata olives and asparagus which make it an absolute veggie blast.

Ingredients:

1. 3 spiralized zucchinis
2. Fresh broccoli florets – 2 cups
3. Chopped artichoke hearts – 1 cup
4. Diced yellow onion – half cup
5. Fresh asparagus tips – 1 cup
6. Halved and pitted kalamata olives – half cup
7. Roughly chopped fresh basil – half cup
8. 5 garlic cloves , sliced
9. 8 roughly chopped sun dried tomatoes
10. Salt – 1 ½ tsp
11. Freshly ground black pepper – ½ tsp
12. Olive oil – 2 tbsp

Method:

• Heat a large frying pan over medium-high heat. Add olive oil, garlic and onions. Sauté for 2 minutes.
• Throw in asparagus, broccoli, sun dried tomatoes, and

artichoke hearts. Stir them well and cover the pan for 2 minutes.
• Add olives, basil, salt and pepper. Stir constantly for 2 minutes.
• Toss in the zucchini ribbons. If the mixture is a bit dry, add a
  tablespoon of water, cover the pan and let the vegetables cook
for 2 minutes, otherwise just cover the pan and let it cook for 2
minutes.

When it's done, divide equally in bowls and eat away!

Sweet Potato Noodles with Coconut Curry and Mango Salsa

This recipe offers refined flavors by bringing together sweet potato noodles with the creamy coconut curry. There is crunch, a smooth creamy flavor, the right balance of spices in the sweetness of mangoes that will make you addicted to this wonderful dish.

Ingredients:
Curry:

1.
 1 spiralized carrot
2.
 1 spiralized red bell pepper
3.
 Chopped onion – 1/3 cup
4.
 Broccoli (cut into bite-sized pieces) – 1 cup
5.
 Coconut oil – half tbsp
6.
 Full fat coconut milk – 3.5 liters
7.
 Freshly minced ginger – 1 tsp

8.

Yellow curry powder – half tbsp

9.

Pinch of salt

Mango salsa:

1.

1 large diced mango – ¾ cup

2.

1 red chili (minced)

3.

Fresh cilantro – ¼ cup (additional for garnish)

4.

Diced red onion – 2 tbsp

5.

Apple cider vinegar – half tsp

6.

Pinch of salt

Sweet potato Noodles:

1.

1 spiralized sweet potato

2.

Coconut oil – half tbsp

3.

Pinch of salt

Method:

• First of all, make the curry. Heat half teaspoon of coconut oil in a medium sauce pan over medium high heat. Throw in the carrots and cook for 2 minutes. Turn the heat to low and add broccoli, pepper, ginger, and onion. Cook for 5 minutes. Add the curry powder and stir constantly for 1 minute. Add the coconut milk and a pinch of salt and mix well. Turn up the heat to medium-high, bring to a boil, and then turn it down to medium-low. Let it simmer for 15 minutes.

• While the sauce is simmering, heat half teaspoon of coconut oil in a separate pan over medium heat. Toss in the potato noodles, season with a pinch of salt and cook for 10 minutes.

• When the noodles are on the stove, combine the ingredients of mango salsa in a medium bowl. Season with a pinch of salt.

• When everything is ready, place the noodles in the bottom of the bowl, top it up with curry and garnish with mango salsa and cilantro.

It is a restaurant quality dish which can blow away your family and friends with a punch of so many diverse flavors in one dish. Enjoy the sweet potato noodles with coconut curry and mango salsa!

Spicy Stir Fry Spaghetti Squash

Full of healthy ingredients and loads of flavor, this lively dish will surely add glamour to your table. It's easy to make and you'd be amazed to see how good it tastes.

Ingredients:

1.
Olive oil – 2 tbsp
2.
¼ chopped red onion
3.
Spaghetti squash spiralized into noodles and cooked – 1 ½ cups
4.
3 ground garlic cloves
5.
Chopped red cabbage – ½ cup
6.
2 small-sized chopped celery stalks
7.
Chili powder – ¼ tsp
8.
Pepper and sea salt, to taste
9.
Cayenne – 1 pinch

10.
Fresh cilantro, torn – 2 tbsp
11.
Fresh avocado

Method:

• Take a large skillet and heat olive oil in it at over medium heat. Add celery, cabbage, peppers and onion in it. Use salt and pepper for seasoning and stir fry the mixture for about 6-7 minutes or until tender.
• Then lower the heat and whisk in the spaghetti squash and remaining spices. Let it cook for another 3-4 minutes.
• Use fresh cilantro for topping and serve the dish with fresh avocado slices.

Chapter 4: casseroles

Zucchini Spinach Lasagna

You might have tasted many different kinds of lasagnas with egg or flour noodles. This lasagna turns zucchini into noodles which will totally knock you out. No heavy feeling afterwards but still the same gooey and cheesy flavor with a vegetable punch.

Ingredients:

1.
 Canned tomatoes – 2 cups
2.
 3 medium-sized zucchinis, spiralized into noodles
3.
 Shredded mozzarella cheese – 1 cup
4.
 Spinach – 4 cups
5.
 Ricotta cheese – 1 ½ cups
6.
 Grated parmesan cheese – 1/3 cup
7.
 1 large egg
8.

Olive oil – 1 tbsp

9.

Red pepper flakes – ¼ tsp

10.

2 garlic cloves

11.

8 basil leaves

12.

Dried oregano flakes – 1 tsp

13.

Chopped red onion – ¾ cup

14.

Salt and pepper – to taste

Method:

- Preheat oven to 400°F.
- Place olive oil in a large pan and put it over medium heat. Add red pepper flakes and crushed garlic and cook for 30 seconds. Toss in the onions and cook for 2 minutes. Then add oregano, basil leaves and canned tomatoes. Season with salt and pepper and keep stirring for 15 minutes until the sauce is reduced. There should be no liquid in the sauce.
- While the sauce is reducing, place a large pan over medium heat and cook the spinach until it is completely wilted. Then cook zucchini noodles in the same pan for 2 minutes after taking out the spinach. Keep tossing them and put them on a colander once they are done. Pat them dry to get out excess moisture.
- Whisk beaten egg, parmesan and ricotta in a bowl.
- Once the sauce is done, take out a casserole dish. Add a layer of tomato sauce, then zucchini noodles, over that ricotta mixture, once again zucchini noodles, and finally the remaining tomato sauce. Top it up with mozzarella cheese.
- Cover the dish with a tinfoil and bake for 40 minutes. After 40 minutes, take out the dish, remove the tinfoil and let it rest for

10 minutes. After that, carefully pour out excess liquid from the dish. Then cut the lasagna and serve immediately.

This mouthwatering dish is worth all the effort.

Sweet Potato Enchilada Casserole

Loaded with vegetables and packed with flavor, this sweet potato enchilada casserole is a must-try recipe. Plus, it has half the amount of carbs, fat, and total calories that are generally packed in regular casseroles.

Ingredients:

1.
 2 spiralized sweet potatoes
2.
 Red enchilada sauce – 2 cups
3.
 Drained and rinsed black beans – 1 can (2 cups)
4.
 Drained corn – 1 can (2 cups)
5.
 Shredded Colby Jack Cheese – ¾ cup
6.
 Half avocado – chopped
7.
 1 chopped green onion
8.

Parsley – for garnish
9.
Salt and pepper – to taste
10.
Sour cream – for serving

Method:

- Preheat oven to 390°F.
- Take a large mixing bowl and add enchilada sauce, beans, and corns. Season with salt and pepper and set aside.
- Lightly spray a casserole dish with cooking spray. Add the spiralized potatoes and pour the sauce mixture over the potatoes. Top it up with cheese. Cover lightly with aluminum foil.
- Bake for 50 minutes. Remove the aluminum foil and bake for 10 more minutes.
- Let it rest for a few minutes then garnish with parsley, avocado, green onions, and sour cream.

It looks good and tastes great!

Root Vegetable Casserole

Root vegetables are easy to spiralize and they look really beautiful in this form. Add some more taste to these veggies, bake them...and you get a nice and hearty casserole.

Ingredients:
For Alfredo Sauce:

1.
Unsweetened almond milk – ¾ cup
2.
Gluten-free Dijon mustard – 2 tbsp
3.
Coarsely chopped raw cashews – 1/3 cup
4.
Nutritional Yeast – 3 tbsp
5.
Half shallot – cut in 2 pieces
6.
Tahini – 1 tbsp
7.
1 chopped garlic clove
8.
Kosher seas salt – ¼ tsp
9.
Gluten-free tamari – 2 tsp
10.

Ground nutmeg – 1/8 tsp

11.

Paprika – ¼ tsp

12.

Butter – 2 tbsp

For Noodles:

1.

2 spiralized sweet potatoes

2.

2 spiralized rutabagas

3.

2 spiralized turnips

Topping:

1.

Dried oregano – half tbsp

2.

2 slices of bread – toasted and finely chopped

Method:

- Preheat oven to 350°F.
- Lightly spray a casserole dish with cooking spray.
- Toast two slices of bread and chop into bread crumbs. Put the crumbs and dried oregano in a large Ziploc bag and shake to mix well.
- Combine all the ingredients of the sauce in a blender and blend until they turn into a smooth mixture.
- Take a bowl, place the spiralized noodles in it, add half of the Alfredo sauce and toss to coat the noodles evenly with sauce.
- Put the spiralized noodles in the casserole dish. Pour the remaining sauce over them. Cover and bake for 30 minutes. Remove the cover, sprinkle the bread crumbs and bake uncovered for 15 more minutes.

- Take out of the oven and let it rest for 10 minutes. Cut into square pieces and serve.

Dig in and enjoy the flavors of this vegetarian casserole!

Carrot Enchilada Casserole

This spicy carrot enchilada casserole combines carrots, beans, veggies and enchilada sauce. It fills you up without weighing you down. Most importantly, it is super tasty.

Ingredients:

1.
 3 spiralized carrots
2.
 Crushed tomatoes – 1 can
3.
 Frozen corn – 1 ¼ cups
4.
 Cooked black beans – 1 can
5.
 Freshly minced cilantro – 2 tsp
6.
 1 red bell pepper – spiralized or diced
7.
 1 diced white onion
8.
 1 minced jalapeno
9.

Fresh lime juice – 1 tbsp
10.
Grated pepper Jack cheese – 1 cup
11.
Olive oil – 1 tbsp
12.
Ground cumin – 2 tsp
13.
Chilli powder – 1 tbsp
14.
Salt and pepper – to taste
15.
Minced garlic – 1 tsp
16.
Dried oregano – half tsp

Method:

- Heat oven to 375°F.
- Coat baking pan with cooking spray.
- Heat olive oil in a large pan over medium heat. Add onion, garlic, and bell pepper. Cook for 2 minutes. Add cumin, corn, chili powder, jalapeno, cilantro, and oregano. Cook until the corn is heated. Season with salt, pepper and lime juice. Cook for 3 minutes. Add carrots and tomatoes. Cook for 2 more minutes. Then empty the contents of this pan into the casserole dish.
- Sprinkle cheese over the casserole, cover with foil and bake for 15 minutes. Then uncover and bake for 10 more minutes.

Serve warm and enjoy the spicy, cheesy and healthy casserole.

Asparagus and Potato Noodle Casserole

This casserole is very delicious and elegant. The creaminess of gruyere cheese, lightness of asparagus and the warmth of potato noodles create a texture that is worth sharing with your loved ones.

Ingredients:

1.
 12 asparagus spears – cut off the bottoms
2.
 2 spiralized white potatoes
3.
 Grated parmigiano-reggiano cheese – 2 tbsp
4.
 Grated gruyere cheese – 2 cups
5.
 Pepper – to taste

Method:

• Preheat oven to 390°F.
• Place half of the potato noodles in a casserole dish. Top it up with 1 cup of gruyere cheese. Spread the cheese evenly. Then spread the rest of the potato noodles and finally, spread the

second cup of gruyere over the noodles. Place the asparagus over the gruyere and press all the asparagus spears. Sprinkle freshly grinded pepper.

• Place the dish in the oven and bake for 30 minutes. Take out the dish, set the oven to broil, sprinkle Parmigiano-Reggiano cheese over the casserole, put it back in the oven, and broil for 2 minutes.

• Slice in 8 square pieces when it's done.

The sophisticated appearance and the classy taste can win over the hearts of your loved ones.

Spiralized Sweet Potato and Apple Enchilada Casserole

It's a comforting family meal filled with apples, sweet potatoes, cheese and Mexican flavors.

Ingredients:

1.
 2 spiralized sweet potatoes
2.
 2 unpeeled and thinly spiralized apples
3.
 Chopped onions – ½ cup
4.
 2 minced garlic cloves
5.
 12 wheat tortillas
6.
 Rinsed and drained corn – 1 can
7.
 Rinsed and drained black beans – 1 can
8.
 Enchilada sauce – 3 cups

9.
Shredded Mexican cheese blend – 2 cups
10.
Chopped cojita cheese – 2 cups
11.
Toppings: green onions, avocado, and sour cream

Method:

- Preheat oven to 390°F.
- Spray casserole dish with cooking spray.
- Put a medium saucepan over medium heat. Add apples, potatoes, garlic and onions. Cook for 5 minutes and set aside.
- Spread ¾ cup of enchilada sauce at the bottom of the casserole dish. Then cover the sauce with tortillas. Then spread half of the corn, black beans, and sweet potato mixture. Add 1/3 of both cheeses. Repeat the layer with tortillas, then sauce, after that, beans, corns, sweet potato mixture, and one third of cheeses. Finally, top with the rest of the tortillas and enchilada sauce.
- Cover the dish with aluminum foil and bake for 30 minutes. Uncover the dish, add the remaining cheeses, and bake for 15 more minutes.
- Let the casserole cool for 10 minutes. Then top with avocado, green onions and sour cream.

Such a delicious casserole is never enough. You'll want more and more!

Butternut Squash and Cheese Casserole

This casserole recipe is special because it is a healthy version of traditional mac and cheese. Sweet butternut squash is covered with creamy cheese sauce and then baked to make a wonderful dish that you will love.

Ingredients:

1.
 2 butternut squashes
2.
 Almond milk – 1 ½ cups
3.
 Grated parmesan cheese – ¼ cup
4.
 Grated Monterey Jack cheese – 1 ½ cups
5.
 Grated sharp white cheddar cheese – 1 ½ cups
6.
 Tapioca flour – 3 tbsp
7.
 Kosher salt – to taste
8.
 Freshly ground black pepper – to taste
9.
 Olive oil

10.
Dijon mustard – 1 tsp
11.
Garlic powder – ¼ tsp
12.
Cayenne pepper – 1/8 tsp
13.
Paprika – ¼ tsp
14.
Almond meal – ¼ cup
15.
Finely chopped fresh thyme – 2 sprigs
16.
Finely chopped fresh parsley – 2 tbsp
17.
Butter – 3 tbsp

Method:
- Preheat oven to 430°F.
- Spiralize the butternut squash into thick noodles. Spread them on a baking sheet, drizzle a little olive oil, season with salt and pepper, and bake for 15 minutes.
- While the noodles are in the oven, melt the butter in a medium saucepan over low heat. Add the tapioca flour and cook for 1 minute. Add the Dijon mustard and almond milk. Mix them until smooth. Cook for 5 minutes. Then add garlic powder, cayenne, salt and pepper. Remove the saucepan from the heat. Slowly add cheddar and Jack cheeses and stir until the sauce is smooth and creamy.
- Take a large bowl and combine the noodles and sauce. Toss it thoroughly and transfer it to a baking dish.
- Take a small bowl and combine almond meal, paprika, parmesan cheese, parsley, and a pinch of salt and pepper. Mix well and dust over the casserole.
- Bake the casserole for 30 minutes, let it rest for 15 minutes

and dig in!

The sweetness of butternut squash is beautifully combined with the spicy and cheesy sauce. No one will notice that it's not the typical mac and cheese because there is no comparison between the two. It's simply lip smacking.

Broccoli and Zucchini Noodle Casserole

The superb and healthy combination of veggies, eggs, cheese and yoghurt is what you need when you want to avoid the bloated feeling you typically get after a full dinner. It's not only tasty, it's also very easy to make.

Ingredients:

1.
 4 unpeeled zucchinis
2.
 Broccoli – 2 cups (chopped into small pieces)
3.
 Stemmed and chopped kale – 2 cups
4.
 Chopped basil leaves – half cup
5.
 4 eggs
6.
 Egg whites – 1 cup
7.
 Plain Greek yoghurt – half cup
8.
 Shredded cheddar cheese – 1 ½ cups
9.
 Salt – 1 tsp

10.
Fresh ground black pepper – to taste

Method:

- Preheat oven to 350°F.
- Spray a baking dish with cooking spray.
- Spiralize the zucchinis into noodles. Place the noodles on a large colander and sprinkle salt over them. Toss them and leave them on the colander for 20 minutes. Toss them again. Then place them on a clean kitchen towel and squeeze to remove as much moisture as possible.
- Take a large bowl and mix egg whites, eggs, yoghurt, and pepper. Then add the dried zucchini noodles, basil, kale and broccoli. Stir in one cup of cheese and mix properly. Pour in the baking dish and sprinkle the remaining cheese over the top. Bake for 45 minutes.

Don't skip the step of drying the zucchini noodles or you will get a watery casserole. Enjoy this healthy casserole. It is one of the best ways to serve veggies to kids. They will love it.

Squash Casserole

This squash casserole is a simple and low-carb dish that is full of delectable flavors. Do try it.

Ingredients:

1.
Spiralized yellow squash – 3 cups
2.
1 egg
3.
Parmesan cheese – ¼ cup
4.
Plain yoghurt – half cup
5.
Salt and pepper – to taste

Method:

• Preheat oven to 325 degree Fahrenheit.
• Place the squash in a large bowl. Beat yoghurt and egg and add into the bowl of squash. Then season with salt and pepper and add cheese. Mix well.
• Butter a baking dish and pour this squash mixture into it.

Sprinkle some cheese over the top. Bake for 40 minutes.

Who doesn't like the cheesy baked vegetables? Just leave all the work and feel the flavor of this squashy casserole.

Beetroot and Feta Casserole

Beetroot and Feta Casserole is a Mediterranean recipe. It is very colorful and packs a variety of flavors from the fresh ingredients, especially the vegetables.

Ingredients:

1.
 2 spiralized beetroots
2.
 A half red onion – spiralized
3.
 1 block of feta cheese (1 cup when grated)
4.
 Yellow cherry tomatoes (halved) – 3/8 cup
5.
 Pitted kalamata olives – 60g
6.
 Red cherry tomatoes (halved) – 3/8 cup
7.,
 Freshly chopped parsley – 3 tbsp
8.
 2 finely chopped garlic cloves
9.
 Vinegar – 1 tbsp

10.
Dried oregano – 1 tsp
11.
Olive oil – 1 tbsp
12.
Salt and pepper – to taste

Method:

• Preheat oven to 400°F.
• Combine all the ingredients in a large bowl, except feta cheese and 1 tbsp of parsley.
• Take a large ovenproof frying pan and place the feta in the centre. Surround it with the beetroot noodle mixture. Cover with aluminum foil and bake for 20 minutes. Garnish with parsley and serve hot.

It's so fresh and tasty that it will become one of your favorite casserole dishes.

Winter soup recipes

Baby marrow soup

Serves 4.
Ingredients:
1 ½ lbs (750 g) baby marrows, grated
1 oz (40 g) margarine
½ oz (15 g) flour
4 cups (1 litre) boiling water
2 oz (54 g)packet cream of chicken soup mix
¾ oz (20 g) margarine
4 Vienna sausages
1 egg yolk
7 oz (200 g) cream
finely chopped dill
Method:
· Melt 40 g margarine in a saucepan. Add flour and stir in. blend in water and soup mix. Simmer for 10 minutes. Melt 20 g margarine in a frying pan.
· Add baby marrows and sauté for 5 minutes, or until tender. Add to soup with sliced Vienna's. Combine egg yolk and cream. Stir into soup, heat through. Season to taste.

TOTAL KILOJOULE COUNT: 6, 390 kJ (1,525 Cal). A portion: 1, 595 kJ (380 Cal).

Beef pea soup

Serves 4.

Ingredients:

14 oz (410 g) cans pea soup

1/3 cup (175 ml) natural yoghurt

4 hot dogs cut into chunks

4 oz (112 g) crumbled cheese

Freshly ground black pepper to taste

Method:

· Combine soup and two soup cans of water in a large pot.

· Simmer and stir in yoghurt. Add hot dogs. Cook, covered, for 5 minutes. Serve sprinkled with cheese and pepper.

TOTAL KILOJOULE COUNT: 7, 095 kJ (1, 695 Cal). A portion: 1, 775 kJ (425 Cal).

Beetroot with beef soup

Serves 6.
Ingredients:
2 onions, chopped
1 stalk celery, diced
Hearty beef stock cube
2 cups (500 ml) water
1 lb (500 g) can beetroot or fresh, diced
¼ cup (60 ml) vinegar
1 garlic clove, crushed
2 tea-spoons (10 ml) white sugar
8 oz (250 g) ground beef
1 cup (250 ml) sour cream
Finely chopped dill
Method:
· Put the onions, celery and stock cube in pot with water. Bring to a boil. Add beets to boiling broth with vinegar, garlic, and sugar.
· Simmer for 40 minutes for fresh beetroot. Bring to a boil for canned beetroot. Form meat into small meatballs. Add to soup. Cook for 5 minutes. Serve with sour cream and dill.
TOTAL KILOJOULE COUNT: 2, 885 kJ (690 Cal). A portion: 480 kJ (115 Cal).

Cabbage and barley soup

Ingredients:

2 oz (50 g) Evergreen dehydrated cabbage

2 table-spoons(30 ml) salad oil

6 rashers streaky bacon, chopped

4 table-spoons(60 ml) Evergreen dehydrated onions

2 oz (50 g) Evergreen dehydrated carrots

2. 5oz (60 g) Evergreen mixed dehydrated vegetables

2 oz (50 g) Evergreen dehydrated potatoes

3 sticks eating celery, sliced

3 litres chicken stock

4 table-spoons (60 ml)pearl barley

salt and freshly ground black pepper to taste

4 table-spoons (60 ml)parsley, freshly chopped

Serves 8.

Method:

· Heat oil, in the pot add chopped bacon and remaining ingredients.

· Bring to the boil then simmer for 1 hour. Serve with thick slices of rye bread and butter.

 TOTAL KILOJOULE COUNT: 6 130 kJ (1, 460 Cal) . A portion: 765 kJ (180 Cal).

Carrot and orange soup

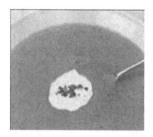

Serves 6-8.
Ingredients:
1 lb and 2 oz (500 g) carrots, diced
1 onion, chopped
½ tea-spoon (3 ml) each thyme
salt and ground black pepper

golden brown sugar

1 oz (30 g) butter
1 cup (250 ml) liquid-fruit orange
2 cups (500 ml) rich chicken stock
Method:
· Sauté carrots, onion, seasoning and butter, leave for 5- 6 minutes. Stir in liquid- fruit and chicken stock. Cover and simmer for 30 minutes, stirring occasionally.
· Puree in a food processor, a little at a time, or press through a sieve. Serve hot topped with a little cream and a sprinkling of chopped parsley.

TOTAL KILOJOULE COUNT: 2, 490 kJ (595 Cal). A portion: 355 kJ (85 Cal).
NOTE: Pumpkin can be combined with, or substituted for carrot.

Cauliflower cheese soup

Serves 4-6.

Ingredients:

1oz (35 g) evergreen dehydrated cauliflower

4 cups (1 litre) milk

2 onions, sliced

2 table-spoons (30 ml) butter

2 table-spoons(30 ml) flour

1 tea-spoon(5 ml) dry mustard

¼ tea-spoon (1 ml)paprika

Pinch of salt

2 table-spoons(30 ml) chopped chives

2 table-spoons (30 ml)cream

4 slices French bread

1 table- spoon(15 ml) butter

4 table-spoons (50 ml)grated cheese

Method:

· Soak cauliflower covered with 750 ml water for 2 hours. Sauté onion in butter in a soup saucepan until limp and beginning to colour.

· Stir in flour until smooth. Add milk and cauliflower, bring to boiling point, stirring continuously. Add mustard, paprika, salt, chives and cream.

· Lightly toast French bread. Butter slices, cover with cheese, place under the grill until golden. Place soup in a bowl . Pour over soup. Serve immediately.

TOTAL KILOJOULE COUNT: 6,325 kJ (1, 510 cal) . A portion: 1, 265 kJ (300 Cal).

Cauliflower soup

Serves 4.
Ingredients:
1 oz (28 g) packet of
creamy mushroom sauce mix

2 cups (500 ml) boiling water
1lb and 2 oz (500 g) frozen or fresh cauliflower flowerets
9 oz (300 g) mushrooms, sliced
1 cup (250 ml) cream or natural yoghurt
Method:
· Add sauce mix to boiling water, whisk until combined. Add cauliflower and mushrooms. Cook until vegetables are tender.
· Puree or press through a sieve and stir in cream. Serve hot.
TOTAL KILOJOULE COUNT: 3, 305 KJ (790 Cal). A portion: 825 kJ (200 Cal).

Cheesy onion soup

Serve 4.

Ingredients:

6 onions, sliced

¼ cup (60 ml) margarine

1 clove garlic, crushed

12 g beef stock cube

2 cups (500 ml) water

½ cup (125 ml) white wine

4 slices bread

1 ½ cups (375 ml) cheese, grated

Method:

· Melt margarine in a large saucepan. Add garlic and onions. Cover and cook over low heat for about 15 minutes to soften.

· Remove lid and cook over high heat, stirring constantly, until onions are caramelized but not brown or crisp. Dissolve stock cube in water.

· Add with wine. Cover and simmer over medium heat for 20 minutes. Place a slice of bread in each of 4 ovenproof soup bowls.

· Top each with 15 ml grated cheese. Ladle hot soup over bread. Sprinkle remaining cheese on top. Bake at 3250F (1600C) for 20 minutes.

TOTAL KILOJOUE COUNT: 6, 790 kJ (1, 625 Cal). A portion: 1, 695 kJ (405 Cal).

Crab soup

Serves 6.
Ingredients:
14 ½ oz (410 g) can tomato soup
14 ½ oz (410 g) pea soup
2 soup cans milk
1 ¼ oz (43 g) can crabmeat
2 table-spoons (30 ml) cream sherry
Method:
Combine all ingredients in soup a pot. Heat through and serve.
TOTAL KILOJOULE COUNT: 4, 725 kJ (1,130 Cal). A portion: 790 kJ
(190 Cal).

Easter fish and vegetable soup

Serves 4-6.

Ingredients:
1 lb (500 g) frozen fish whiting fillets
12 g or 1 cube rich chicken stock cube
4 cups (1 litre) boiling water
1 cup (250 ml) slices mushrooms
1 cup (250 ml) fresh or frozen peas
2 carrots, sliced
½ cup (125 ml) sliced celery
Ground ginger to taste
1 table-spoon (15 ml) soy sauce
Salt and freshly ground black pepper to taste
Method:
· Thaw frozen fish slightly, so that it is easy to cut, and then slice into 2, 5 cm cubes. Dissolve chicken stock cube in boiling water, then add vegetables and seasoning.
· Simmer covered, for 10 minutes. Add fish and simmer 5- 7 minutes, or until fish flakes easily.
TOTAL KILOJOULE COUNT: 5, 210 kJ (1, 245 Cal). A portion: 1, 040 kJ (250 Cal).

Goulash soup

Serves 4-6.

Ingredients:

1lb(500 g) shin, deices
1 table-spoon(15ml) paprika
6 bacon rinds
4 oz (125 g) mixed vegetables
2 table-spoon(30ml) salad oil
4 cups (1 litre) chicken stock
2 oz (50 g) potatoes
2 cloves of garlic, crushed
1 tea-spoon(5ml) mixed herbs
Pinch of salt and freshly
ground black pepper to taste

4 table-spoons(60ml) chopped fresh parsley

Method:

· Heat oil in a saucepan, sauté meat, add paprika and bacon rinds. Stir together a low heat for a few minutes, add remaining ingredients except parsley.
· Cook gently for 2-3 hours. Add parsley. Serve as main dish with sliced whole wheat bread and butter, followed with slices of cheese and bowl of apples or fresh pears.
TOTAL KILOJOULE COUNT: 5, 245 kJ (1, 250 Cal). A portion: 1, 050 kJ (250 Cal).

Great bean soup

Serves 6- 8.

Ingredients:

1 ¾ lbs (795 g) can tomatoes

12 g rich chicken or spicy stock cube

2 cups (500 ml) boiling water

½ tea-spoon (2 ml) pre-packed Italian or Hungarian seasoning

½ tea-spoon (2 ml) chilli powder

14 ½ oz (410 g) can butter beans

14 ½ oz (410 g) can butter beans in tomato sauce

14 ½ oz (410 g) can green beans

Method:

Combine tomatoes with their juice, chicken stock dissolved in boiling water and seasoning in a large saucepan. Bring to boil. Drain canned beans. Add to soup. Heat through, stirring occasionally.

TOTAL KILOJOULE COUNT: 5, 420 kJ (1, 295 Cal). A portion: 775 kJ (185 Cal).

Mussel soup

Serves 4.

Ingredients:

3 oz (90 g) packet cream of tomato soup mix

3 1/3 cups (850 ml) milk

4 oz (105 g) can mussels

1 clove garlic, crushed

salt and freshly ground

black pepper to taste

1 cup (250 ml) natural yoghurt

Method:

Combine soup mix and milk in a saucepan. Whisk until well combined. Heat to boiling simmer for 4 minutes. Add mussels, garlic, salt and pepper. Heat through. Serve with yoghurt.

TOTAL KILOJOULE COUNT: 4, 455 kJ (1, 065 Cal). A portion: 1, 110 kJ (265 Cal).

Leek and vegetable soup

Serves 4- 6.
Ingredients:
4 leeks thinly sliced
2 stalks table celery, thinly sliced
4 table-spoons(60 ml) butter
2 cups (500 ml) water
2 potatoes, sliced
pinch of salt and freshly ground black pepper to taste
3 cups (750 ml) milk
4 table-spoons (60 ml)thick cream
Method:
· In a heavy saucepan, gently cook leeks and celery in butter, covered, for about 20 minutes. Add water, potatoes, salt and freshly ground black pepper. Simmer mixture for 45 minutes. Add milk and cream, cook soup for 15 minutes.
· Serve with slices of toasted cheese.
TOTAL KILOJOULE COUNT: 6, 285 kJ (1, 500 Cal). A portion: 1, 255 kJ (300 Cal).

Lemon soup

Serves 4.

Ingredients:
2 table-spoon (30 ml) melted margarine
1 cup (250 ml) onion, finely minced
1 tea-spoon (5 ml) salt
Freshly ground black pepper to taste
1 cup (250 ml) cooked rice
½ cup (100 ml) lemon juice
2 cups (500 ml) boiling water
½ oz (12 g)rich chicken stock cube
2 eggs, beaten
 1 tea-spoon (5 ml)crushed mint
Chopped parsley and cream to garnish
Method:
· Heat margarine in a soup pot. Sauté onion with salt and pepper until onion is soft and transparent. Add rice, stock cube dissolved in water and lemon juice.
· Heat until boiling. Gradually pour in eggs, beating rapidly. Add mint. Remove from heat, garnish with parsley and cream and serve.
TOTAL KILOJOULE COUNT: 4 790 kJ(1, 145 Cal). A portion: 1, 195 kJ(285 Cal).

Lemony mushroom soup

Serves 4.

Ingredients:

1 oz (30 g) margarine

1 onion, sliced

1 ¼ lbs (500 g) button mushrooms

2 cups (500 ml) boiling water

12 g rich chicken stock cube

1 ½ cups (400 ml) skimmed milk

1 tea-spoon (5 ml) salt

Freshly ground black pepper to taste

1 lemon

1 tea-spoon (5 ml) white sugar

Method:

· Melt margarine in saucepan and sauté onion until soft. Add mushrooms and continue sautéing for 5 minutes.

· Stir in boiling water in which stock cube has been dissolved. Add milk and seasoning. Cover and simmer for 25 minutes. Puree soup.

· Cut lemon in half. Add juice and grated peel of ½ lemon and sugar to soup. Heat through. Slice remaining half lemon thinly and float slices in soup.

TOTAL KILOJOULE COUNT: 2, 465 kJ (590 Cal). A portion: 615 kJ (145 Cal).

Meadow soup

Serves 4.

Ingredients:

1 ¼ lbs (500 g) mixed frozen vegetables

1 large onion, diced

4 table-spoons (60 ml) margarine

2 table-spoon (15 ml) flour

3 cups (750 ml) chicken stock

Salt and freshly ground black pepper to taste

2 cups (500 ml) milk

2 table-spoons (30 ml) freshly chopped parsley

Method:

· Melt margarine in a large saucepan and sauté onion until tender. Add vegetables, cover and cook for about 5 minutes.

· Add flour and stir well. Gradually add chicken stock, stirring constantly. Cover and simmer gently until vegetables are tender.

· Add seasoning to taste and add enough milk to give the desired consistency. Sprinkle with parsley and serve.

TOTAL KILOJOULE COUNTS: 5, 015 kJ (1, 195 Cal). Per portion: 1, 255 kJ (300 Cal).

Minted pea soup

Serves 3-4.
Ingredients:
14 ¾ oz (410 g) can peas
1 onion finely chopped
1 tablespoon (15 ml) salad oil
1 ½ cups (375 ml) milk
½ cup (120 ml) water
Salt and freshly ground black pepper to taste
½ cup (125 ml)cream

For Garnish:

1 table-spoon(15 ml) chopped mint leaves
Croutons fried bread or crumbled fried bacon
Method:
• Fry onion in oil until soft. Drain and place in a blender with drained peas, milk, water, seasoning and cream. Blend at top speed until smooth.
• Sieve if necessary. Reheat gently or chill and serve garnished with chopped mint and croutons.
TOTAL KILOJOULE COUNT: 6, 360 kJ (1, 495 Cal). Per portion: 1, 790 kJ (425 Cal).

Mussels with yoghurt soup

Serves 4.
Ingredients:
3 oz (90 g) cream of tomato soup mix
6 1/3 cups (850 ml) milk
4 oz (105 g) can mussels
1 clove garlic, crushed
Salt and freshly ground black pepper to taste
1 cup (250 ml) natural yoghurt
 Method:
· Combine soup mix and milk in a saucepan. Whisk until well combined. Heat to boiling, simmer for 4 minutes.
· Add mussels, garlic, salt and pepper. Heat through. Serve with yoghurt.
TOTAL KILOJOULE COUNTS: 4, 455 kJ (1,065 Cal). A portion: 1,110 kJ (265 Cal).

Onion carrot soup

Serve 6.
Ingredients:
2 lbs (1 kg) carrots, grated
Chicken stock cube
2 cups (500 ml) water
½ tea-spoon (2 ml) nutmeg
½ tea-spoon (2 ml)curry powder
1 cup (250 ml) sour cream
Pinch of salt
2 onions, diced
Sprinkle ground nutmeg
Method:
Combine carrots, stock cube, water and spices into pot. Bring to a boil, add sour cream and salt. Stir in onions. When is cooked serve sprinkle with nutmeg.
 TOTAL KILOJOULE COUNT: 3, 264 (780 Cal). A portion: 545 kJ (130 Cal).

Peanut squash soup

Serves 4.
Ingredients:
2 lbs (1 kg) butternut squash
12 g spicy curry stock cube (1 cube)
4 cups (1 litre) boiling water
1 apple cut into eights
1 onion, quartered
½ cup (125 ml) peanut butter
2 tea-spoons (10 ml) white sugar
½ cup (125 ml) cream or natural yoghurt
Method:
· Peel and seed squash. Cut into 5 cm, pieces. Dissolve stock cube in boiling water. Add squash, apple and onion. Cover and simmer for 20 minutes, or until tender.
· Stir in peanut butter. Puree soup, a little at a time. Return to pot and stir in cream or yoghurt. Heat gently.
TOTAL KILOJOULE COUNT: 7, 120 kJ (1, 700 Cal). A portion: 1, 780 kJ (425 Cal).

Quick fish soup

Serves 4.
Ingredients:
1 ¼ lbs (500 g) any fish fillets
2 onions
1 table-spoon (15 ml) margarine
1 lb (410 g) can tomatoes
1 turnip, grated (optional)
2 1/3 cups (600 ml) water
8 oz (225 g) mussels or baby clams
Salt and pepper to taste
½ tea-spoon (2 ml) dried herbs
Chopped dill to garnish
Method:
• Cut fish into pieces. Peel and slice onions, then sauté in margarine. Add fish pieces, tomatoes with their liquid and stock. Simmer, covered, for 10 minutes.
• Add mussels with their juice. Season with salt, pepper and dill.
TOTAL KILOJOULE COUNT: 3, 310 kJ (790 Cal). A portion: 825 kJ (200 Cal).

Rice and vegetable soup

Serves 4.

Ingredients:

½ cup (250 ml) long grain white rice
2 table-spoons (30 ml) salad oil
3 cups (750 ml) chicken stock cube diluted with water
2 carrots, grated
½ turnip, grated
1 potato, grated
2 oz (60 g) celery, diced
2 oz (60 g) cucumber, sliced
1 bunch parsley, chopped
Soy sauce and white pepper to taste

Method:

· Sauté rice in oil until well coated. Add chicken stock. Bring to a boil then simmer, covered, for 15 minutes. Vegetables, parsley and seasonings.
· Continue simmering until vegetables are tender. TOTAL KILOJOULE COUNT: 4 100 kJ (980 Cal). A portion: 1 025 kJ (245 Cal).

Rice with cheese soup

Serve 4.
Ingredients:
2/3 cup (150 ml) long-grained white rice
2 table-spoons (30 ml) margarine
4 cups (1 litre) water
rich chicken stock cubes
1 leek finely chopped
2 eggs beaten
2 oz (45 ml) Elite Gouda cheese, grated
2 tea-spoons (10 ml) nutmeg
Salt and freshly ground black pepper to taste
2 oz (50 g) Parmesan cheese, grated
Chopped parsley to garnish
Method:
· Sauté rice lightly, stirring in, margarine over medium heat. Add water and bring to the boil. Add crumbled stock cubes and stir until dissolved.
· Add leek. Cover and simmer for 20 minutes. Combine eggs. Gouda cheese and seasoning. Beat mixture into simmering stock. Remove from heat.
· Ladle into soup bowls and top with Parmesan cheese and parsley.
TOTAL KILOJOULE COUNT: 4, 150 kJ (990 Cal). A portion: 1, 035 kJ (250 Cal).

Tomato soup

Server-4-6

Ingredients:
1 oz (435 g) can condensed tomato soup
2 cups (500 ml) Liquid- fruit Orange
Freshly ground black pepper
Orange slices to garnish
Method:
Combine soup and juice, stirring until smooth and well blended. Season to taste with pepper. Chill, serve cold, topped with orange slices.
TOTAL KILOJOULE: 5 180 kJ (1, 240 Cal). A portion: 1, 035 kJ (250 Cal).

Vegetable beef soup

Serves 4.
Ingredients:
14 ½ oz (500 g) beef brisket
4 cups (1,25 litres) water
2 tea-spoon (10 ml) salt
Freshly ground black pepper to taste
1 table-spoon (15 ml) soy sauce
2 carrots
1 parsnip
2 leeks
3 stalks celery
1 onion
1 clove
4 ½ oz (125 g) peas
Chopped parsley to garnish(optional)
Method:
· Place beef in cold water and bring to boil. Skim fat off. Add salt, pepper and soy sauce. Simmer, covered, for 45 minutes.
· Trim vegetables and dice. Add all but onion to broth and continue simmering for 30 minutes.
· Brown onion and clove and add, with peas, to soup after 15 minutes. Remove meat. Dice and return to soup. Sprinkle with parsley and serve.
TOTAL KILOJOULE COUNT: A portion: 1, 570 kJ (375 Cal).

Part 2

Macaroni-and-'Cheese' Casserole

Cooking time: **20 minutes**

Servings: 4-6

Ingredients:

- 3 ½ cups elbow macaroni
- 4 cups water
- 3 ½ cup boiling water
- ½ cup vegan margarine
- ½ cup flour
- 2 tablespoons soy sauce
- 1 ½ teaspoon garlic powder
- ½ teaspoon paprika
- ¼ cup vegetable oil
- 1 cup nutritional yeast
- A pinch of turmeric
- Salt, to taste

Instructions:
1. Preheat the oven to 350F.
2. Bring water to a boil in a medium sauce pan. Cook macaroni as per package instructions. Drain.
3. Preheat margarine in a pan over low heat until melted. Add flour, whisk well to combine.
4. Continue cooking until smooth, stirring constantly.

5. Add 3 ½ cup boiling water, soy sauce, garlic powder, paprika, turmeric and salt. Stir until combined.
6. Add oil and nutritional yeast. Add pasta and toss well to coat. Transfer to a casserole dish.
7. Bake for 15 minutes and then broil for 1-2 minutes until crisp.

Nutritional info (per serving): 289 calories; 7 g fat; 45 g carbohydrate; 10 g protein

Mashed Potatoes with Roasted Garlic

Cooking time: **35 minutes**

Servings: 4

Ingredients:

- 4 potatoes, peeled and quartered
- 1 garlic head
- 1 teaspoon olive oil
- 4 tablespoons vegan butter
- ½ cup soy milk
- Fresh chives
- Salt, pepper, to taste

Instructions:

1. Preheat the oven to 430F.
2. Peel the outer layer of garlic head, chop off the tips of the garlic. Wrap in foil and drizzle with olive oil. Close the foil and bake for 35 minutes.
3. Add potatoes to the pot and cover with water. Bring to a boil and cook for 20-25 minutes.
4. Drain water let rest for 2-3 minutes.
5. Add vegan butter and mash potatoes with a masher.
6. Add soy milk, ¼ cup at a time and mashing it in, until smooth.
7. Pop the cloves of the garlic out, mash with a fork. Add to potatoes.

8. Add salt and black pepper to taste. Serve topped with fresh chives.

Nutritional info (per serving): 333 calories; 9.2 g fat; 56 g carbohydrate; 6.6 g protein

Blueberry Pancakes

Cooking time: **30 minutes**

Servings: 15-20

Ingredients:

- 2 cups flour
- 3 tablespoons sugar
- 1 tablespoon baking powder
- 3 tablespoons coconut oil
- 2 cups soy or almond milk
- ½ cup fresh or frozen blueberries
- ½ teaspoon salt

Instructions:

1. Mix flour, sugar, baking powder and salt in a bowl.
2. Add milk and oil and mix well until combined. Add blueberries and stir to combine.
3. Preheat a non stick pan over medium heat, pour about 1-2 tablespoons of batter to a skillet. Cook for about 3 minutes per side.
4. Serve topped with syrup or fruits.

Nutritional info (per serving): 159 calories; 3 g fat; 30 g carbohydrate; 4 g protein

Vegetable Lasagna

Cooking time: **1 hour**

Servings: 8

Ingredients:

- 1 box lasagna noodles
- 4 ½ cups jarred marinara
- 1 cup cashew ricotta
- 1 ½ cups fresh spinach
- 2 ½ cups mixed vegetables, chopped, fresh
- ½ cup vegan parmesan cheese

Instructions:

1. Preheat the oven to 375F. Mix spinach and ricotta in a bowl.
2. Spread about 2 cups sauce on the bottom of a baking dish.
3. Add raw lasagna noodles, top with more sauce.
4. Add veggies on top and more lasagna noodles. Sprinkle with half of Parmesan. Top with the remaining noodles.
5. Top with the remaining sauce. Add the remaining Parmesan on top.
6. Cover with foil and bake for 45 minutes. Remove foil and bake for 15 minutes more. Let cool before serving.

Nutritional info (per serving): 433 calories; 9 g fat; 32 g carbohydrate; 14 g protein

Creamy Vegan Zucchini Casserole

Cooking time: **30 minutes**

Servings: 4-6

Ingredients:

- 3 zucchini, sliced
- 2 cups cherry tomatoes, halved
- 1 cup creamy vegan cheese
- ¼ cup fresh basil, chopped
- 4 garlic cloves, crushed
- 2 tablespoons olive oil
- ¼ teaspoon smoked paprika
- 1 pinch cayenne pepper
- Salt, pepper, to taste

Instructions:

1. Preheat the oven to 375F. Mix zucchini, garlic, basil, olive oil, smoked paprika, salt and pepper in a bowl. Mix well to coat zucchini.
2. Spread zucchini mixture on the bottom of a baking dish.
3. Spread vegan cheese on top of zucchini layer. Repeat layers until all the ingredients are used. Top with the cherry tomatoes and the final layer of cheese.
4. Season with cayenne pepper. Bake for about 30 minutes.

Nutritional info (per serving): 293 calories; 24.2 g fat; 14.7 g carbohydrate; 6.7 g protein

Avocado Cream Pasta

Cooking time: **30 minutes**

Servings: 4-6

Ingredients:

- 2 avocados, pitted and diced
- 2 cups pasta of choice, cooked
- 1 garlic clove, minced
- ½ lemon, juiced
- ¼ cup unsweetened soy milk
- ¼ cup water
- 4 cherry tomatoes, halved
- Salt, to taste
- A pinch of red pepper flakes

Instructions:

1. Add avocado, garlic and lemon juice to a food processor or a blender. Process until smooth.

2. Add soy milk and water. Add salt and red pepper. Process until combined.
3. Pour sauce over pasta and toss well to coat, serve.

Nutritional info (per serving): 639 calories; 33 g fat; 77 g carbohydrate; 14 g protein

Apple Muffins with Cinnamon

Cooking time: **25 minutes**

Servings: 12

Ingredients:

- 1 tablespoon ground flax
- 3 tablespoons water
- 3 cups whole wheat flour
- 2 teaspoons baking powder
- ½ cup sugar
- A pinch salt
- 2 teaspoons vanilla extract
- 1 cup non-dairy milk
- ½ cup lemon juice
- ½ cup unsweetened apple juice
- ½ cup apples, peeled, chopped
- 1 ½ teaspoons ground cinnamon
- 3 tablespoons coconut oil
- 3 tablespoons rolled oats
- 3 tablespoons walnuts, chopped

Instructions:

1. Preheat the oven to 400F. Prepare the muffin tins and grease with cooking spray.
2. Mix cinnamon, oil, rolled oats and walnuts in a bowl. Set aside.
3. Mix ground flax and water in a separate bowl. Add flour, baking powder, sugar and salt, mix well to combine.
4. Mix vanilla, milk, apple juice and lemon juice in a bowl. Add dry mixture to the wet mixture and stir well to combine.
5. Pour the batter into muffin tins, top with cinnamon mixture. Bake for 25 minutes. Let cool before serving.

Nutritional info (per serving): 155 calories; 4.9 g fat; 26.8 g carbohydrate; 1.5 g protein

Vegan Shepherd's Pie

Cooking time: 1 hour 20 minutes

Servings: 8

Ingredients:

- 2 ½ lbs King Edward potatoes
- 2 tablespoons vegetable oil
- 2 tablespoons dried porcini mushrooms, soaked in hot water for 15 mins, drained
- 2 leeks, chopped
- 2 onions, chopped
- 4 celery ribs, chopped
- 14 oz canned chickpeas
- 8 oz frozen peas
- 8 oz fresh spinach
- 1 butternut squash, peeled and cut into cubes
- 2 tablespoons tomato purée
- 4 carrots, cut into cubes
- 1 vegetable stock cube
- 3 garlic cloves, crushed
- 2 teaspoons smoked paprika
- 1 tablespoon fresh oregano, chopped
- ½ teaspoon thyme
- 1 teaspoon sage leaves, chopped

- 2 tablespoons olive oil
- Salt, pepper, to taste

Instructions:

1. Add potatoes (unpeeled) to a sauce pan and cover with water. Bring to a boil and cook for 40 minutes. Drain and let cool.
2. Preheat vegetable oil in a pan and add mushrooms, leeks , onions, carrots and stock cube, cook for 5 minutes. Stir occasionally.
3. Add garlic, tomato purée, paprika, squash, oregano, thyme and sage. Stir well and cook for 3 minutes. Add celery and cook for 2 minutes more.
4. Add chickpeas with canned water, spinach and stir well. Cook for 5 minutes, season with salt and pepper.
5. Peel the potatoes and mash with a fork. Add about 1 cup of potatoes to vegetables, mix the rest with olive oil and season with salt and pepper.
6. Transfer everything to a pie pan and top with mashed potatoes. Preheat the oven to 375F. Bake for 40-45 minutes. Serve with vegan tomato ketchup.

Nutritional info (per serving): 396 calories; 5.3 g fat; 72 g carbohydrate; 17.7 g protein

Moroccan Spiced Cauliflower and Almond Soup

Cooking time: **25 minutes**

Servings: 4

Ingredients:

- 1 large cauliflower head, cut into small florets
- 2 tablespoons olive oil
- 2 tablespoons harissa paste
- ½ teaspoon cinnamon
- ½ teaspoon cumin
- ½ teaspoon coriander
- 4 cups hot vegetable stock
- 2 tablespoons toasted flaked almond

Instructions:
1. Preheat oil in a non stick pan. Add cinnamon, coriander and cumin, stir once and add paste. Cook for 2 minutes.
2. Add cauliflower florets, almonds and stock. Cover the pan and cook for 20 minutes.
3. Let cool a little. Transfer soup to a blender and process until smooth. Serve topped with almonds.

Nutritional info (per serving): 116 calories; 8 g fat; 9 g carbohydrate; 4 g protein

Tofu Popcorn Chick'n

Cooking time: **15 minutes**

Servings: 8

Ingredients:

- 13 oz extra firm tofu
- ⅓ cup chickpea flour
- ¼ cup nutritional yeast
- 1 tablespoon mustard
- 1 teaspoon Cajun seasoning
- 1 teaspoon salt
- ½ teaspoon pepper
- ½ cup water
- 3 tablespoons extra virgin olive oil

Instructions:

1. Put something heavy on top of tofu, press for 10 minutes. Drain and set aside.
2. Mix flour, nutritional yeast, Cajun seasoning, salt and pepper in a bowl.
3. Add water slowly and whisk well until combined.
4. Add mustard and mix well. Break tofu into big chunks. Add to the flour mixture and toss well to coat.
5. Preheat oil in a non stick pan. Add tofu mixture to the pan and cook on all sides until golden. Serve.

Nutritional info (per serving): 132 calories; 8.4 g fat; 8.7 g carbohydrate; 8.1g protein

Cauliflower Hot Wings

Cooking time: **50 minutes**

Servings: 4

Ingredients:

- 1 cauliflower head, broken into florets
- ¾ cup flour
- ¾ cup almond milk, unsweetened
- ¼ cup water
- ¾ cup breadcrumbs
- 1 cup spicy BBQ sauce
- 2 teaspoons garlic powder
- 1 ½ teaspoons paprika
- 1 teaspoon Sriracha sauce
- 2 green onions, sliced
- Salt, pepper, to taste

Instructions:

1. Preheat the oven to 350F. Line a baking sheet with parchment paper.
2. Mix flour, milk, water, garlic power, paprika, salt, and black pepper in a bowl.

3. Dip the cauliflower florets into the flour milk mixture, coat well.
4. Dip them into panko breadcrumbs.
5. Lay the cauliflower florets on the baking sheet in one layer. Bake for 25 minutes.
6. Transfer the cooked cauliflower wings to a bowl. Mix BBQ sauce and sriracha sauce, pour it over the cauliflower wings. Coat them from all sides.
7. Put the coated hot wings back on the baking sheet and bake again for 20 minutes.
8. Serve topped with green onions. Enjoy!

Nutritional info (per serving): 388 calories; 12.4 g fat; 63.1 g carbohydrate; 8 g protein

Falafel Burgers

Cooking time: **6 minutes**

Servings: 4

Ingredients:

- 1 can (14 oz) chickpeas, rinsed and drained
- 1 red onion, chopped
- 1 garlic clove, chopped
- 1 teaspoon ground cumin
- 1 teaspoon ground coriander
- ½ teaspoon chilli powder
- 2 tablespoons flour
- 2 tablespoons sunflower oil
- 7 oz tomato salsa
- Green salad, for serving
- Pita bread, toasted, for serving
- A handful parsley

Instructions:

1. Add chickpeas, onion, garlic, parsley, cumin, coriander, chilli powder and flour to a food processor. Blend until smooth.
2. Form medium sized patties out of the mixture. Preheat oil in a frying pan over medium heat.
3. Add patties and cook for about 3 minutes on each side.
4. Serve on toasted pita bread, with tomato salsa and salad.

Nutritional info (per serving): 161 calories; 8 g fat; 18 g carbohydrate; 6 g protein

Minty Pea and Potato Soup

Cooking time: **25 minutes**

Servings: 4

Ingredients:

- 2 lbs potatoes, peeled, cubed
- 1 onion, chopped
- 2 teaspoons vegetable oil
- 4 cups vegetable stock
- 1 ½ cups frozen peas
- A handful fresh mint, chopped
- Salt, pepper, to taste

Instructions:

1. Preheat oil in a large saucepan over medium heat. Add onion and cook for about 4-5 minutes until soft.
2. Add potatoes and stock, bring to the boil. Cover the pan and simmer for 10-15 minutes.
3. In the last 2 minutes of cooking add peas.
4. Let the soup cool a little, then transfer to a blender (or you can use immersion blender instead). Blend until smooth.
5. Season to taste and serve topped with mint.

Nutritional info (per serving): 249 calories; 3 g fat; 48 g carbohydrate; 11 g protein

Chickpea, Tomato and Spinach Curry

Cooking time: **40 minutes**

Servings: 6

Ingredients:

- 1 onion, chopped
- 6 tomatoes
- 1 broccoli head, broken into small florets
- 1 can (14 oz) chickpeas, drained
- ½ cup baby spinach leaves
- 2 garlic cloves, chopped
- 1 ¼ inch piece ginger, grated
- ½ tablespoon oil
- 1 teaspoon ground cumin
- 2 teaspoons ground coriander
- 1 teaspoon turmeric
- 1 teaspoon yeast
- 4 tablespoons red lentils
- 6 tablespoons coconut cream
- 1 lemon, juiced
- 1 tablespoon toasted sesame seeds
- 1 tablespoon chopped cashew

Instructions:

1. Add onion, garlic, ginger and tomatoes to a blender or a food processor. Blend until pureed.
2. Preheat oil in a pan over medium heat. Add all the spices and cook for 1 minute, add puree and yeast. Cook for about 2 minutes until bubbly.
3. Add lentils and coconut cream, cook until lentils are soft. Add broccoli and cook for 4 minutes more.
4. Add chickpeas and spinach, add lemon juice, sesame seeds and cashew. Stir well to combine. Serve over rice.

Nutritional info (per serving): 204 calories; 7 g fat; 20 g carbohydrate; 11 g protein

Vegan Garlic Buffalo Brussels Sprouts

Cooking time: **35 minutes**

Servings: 6

Ingredients:

- 16 oz Brussels sprouts, ends trimmed
- 3 cups Panko bread crumbs
- 1 cup almond milk
- 1 teaspoon apple cider vinegar
- ¾ cup all purpose flour
- ½ cup corn starch
- 2 teaspoon hot sauce
- ½ cup hot sauce
- ½ cup vegan butter
- 1 tablespoon agave syrup
- 1 teaspoon soy sauce
- 8 garlic cloves, chopped
- Salt, to taste

Instructions:

1. Preheat the oven to 425F.

2. Mix almond milk and apple cider vinegar in a bowl. Let rest for about a minute.
3. Mix flour, cornstarch and salt in a separate bowl. Whisk 2 teaspoons of hot sauce to the almond milk mixture, pour the mixture on top of flour mixture and stir well. Whisk until fully combined.
4. Dip each Brussels sprout first in batter and then in Panko breadcrumbs. Spread on a sheet pan layered with parchment paper.
5. Bake for 10 minutes, flip each sprout and bake for another 10-15 minutes.
6. Meanwhile, cook the sauce. Preheat began butter in a skillet over medium heat. Add garlic and cook for 2 minutes. Add hot sauce, agave, say sauce. Cook for 1 minute more.
7. Serve cooked sprouts with the sauce.

Nutritional info (per serving): 406 calories; 12.8 g fat; 64.9 g carbohydrate; 11.2 g protein

Spring Rolls with Carrot-Ginger Dipping Sauce

Cooking time: **55 minutes**

Servings: 6

Ingredients:

- 6 rice-paper wrappers
- 2 cups radish sprouts (1/2 ounce)
- 1 red beet, trimmed and thinly sliced crosswise
- 1 medium carrot, peeled and julienned
- 1 cucumber, julienned
- 1 red bell pepper, stem and seeds removed, julienned
- 3/4 cup coarsely grated daikon
- 3 medium carrots, peeled and coarsely chopped
- 1 small shallot, quartered
- 2 tablespoons coarsely grated peeled fresh ginger
- 1/4 cup rice-wine vinegar (not seasoned)
- 2 tablespoons low-sodium soy sauce
- 1/4 teaspoon toasted sesame oil
- salt and freshly ground pepper, to taste
- 1/4 cup vegetable oil
- 1/4 cup water

Instructions:

To make the spring rolls:

1. Soak one rice-paper wrapper in a large bowl of hot water until pliable. Transfer to a work surface.
2. Place one-sixth of the sprouts, beet slices, carrot, cucumber, bell pepper, and daikon on the wrapper, towards the bottom. Fold ends in and roll tightly to enclose filling.
3. Repeat with remaining ingredients to make 5 more rolls.
4. To make the dipping sauce:
5. Puree carrots, shallot, ginger, vinegar, soy sauce, sesame oil, salt, and pepper in a food processor until smooth.
6. With machine running, add vegetable oil and then water through the feed tube in a slow, steady stream.
7. Serve sauce with spring rolls.

Nutritional info (per serving): 120 calories; 9.4 g fat; 9 g carbohydrate; 1.5 g protein

Corn Potato Chowder

Cooking time: 20 minutes

Servings: 4

Ingredients:

- 4 medium or large potatoes, peeled and diced
- 2 carrots, chopped
- 1 onion, chopped
- 2 stalks celery, chopped
- 2 garlic cloves, minced
- 3 cups water or vegetable broth
- 3 cups almond or soy milk
- 1 cup fresh or frozen corn kernels
- 1 tablespoon olive oil
- ¼ cup flour
- 3 tablespoons nutritional yeast
- ½ teaspoon dried oregano
- ½ teaspoon dried thyme
- Salt, pepper, to taste

Instructions:

1. Preheat oil in a big pot over medium heat. Add onions and cook for 2 minutes. Add garlic, carrots and celery, sauté for 4-5 minutes.

2. Add flour, oregano and thyme, mix well. Sauté for couple of minutes to coat the vegetables with flour, until flour starts turning brown.
3. Add potatoes, broth, milk and nutritional yeast, mix well. Bring soup to a boil and cook over medium heat for about 10 minutes until potatoes are soft.
4. After that add corn, salt and pepper to taste and cook for 2 more minutes. Turn off the heat and serve!

Nutritional info (per serving): 176 calories; 3 g fat; 31 g carbohydrate; 5 g protein

Spicy Carrot Soup

Cooking time: 40 minutes

Servings: 4

Ingredients:

- 10-12 big carrots, peeled and chopped
- 1 onion, chopped
- 2 garlic cloves, crushed
- 1 tablespoon coconut oil
- 1 can (14 oz) coconut milk
- 3 teaspoons red curry paste
- 4 cups vegetable stock or water
- 1/3 cup peanut butter
- Salt, pepper, to taste

Instructions:

1. Heat coconut oil in a big pot over medium heat. Add onions and cook for 3 minutes until soften. Add red curry paste and garlic, cook for 1 more minutes stirring well.
2. Add stock or water, milk and carrots. Bring soup to a boil, reduce the heat to low and cook covered for 25-30 minutes.
3. Add peanut butter, salt and pepper, mix well. Use blender to puree the soup until smooth.
4. Add more salt and pepper if needed and serve.

Nutritional info (per serving): 238 calories; 7 g fat; 34 g carbohydrate; 11 g protein

Hummus Pizza with Veggies

Cooking time: 20 minutes

Servings: 6-8

Ingredients:

- 3 ½ cups flour
- 8-10 mushrooms, sliced
- 1 cup hummus
- 1 teaspoon salt
- 1 teaspoon instant yeast
- 1 pinch sugar
- 3 tablespoons olive oil
- 1 cup warm water
- 1 handful fresh spinach
- ½ cup black olives
- ½ cup artichoke hearts in oil, chopped
- ½ cup cherry tomatoes, halved
- ½ red onion, sliced
- 2 teaspoons dried oregano
- Red pepper flakes, to taste

Instructions:

1. Mix flour, salt, yeast and sugar in a bowl. Add oil and water. Knead with your hands until smooth dough is formed.
2. Form into a ball and cover with plastic wrap. Let rest in a warm place for about an hour, until doubles in size.
3. Preheat the oven to 350F.
4. Transfer the dough to a working surface, dusted with flour. Divide into two balls and form into two pizzas.
5. Spread hummus on top of pizzas, add olives, spinach, artichoke, tomatoes and onion on top. Season with oregano and red pepper flakes. Bake for 20 minutes.

Nutritional info (per serving): 423 calories; 13.1 g fat; 65.2 g carbohydrate; 12.2 g protein

Mushroom Creamy Soup

Cooking time: 10 minutes

Servings: 4

Ingredients:

- 2 lb mushrooms, sliced
- 1 onion, chopped
- 2 garlic cloves, chopped
- 5 cups almond milk or any other plant milk
- 3 cups vegetable stock
- 1 teaspoon ground ginger
- 1 teaspoon lemon juice
- 2 tablespoons fresh parsley, chopped
- Salt, pepper, to taste

Instructions:

1. Put mushrooms, onion and garlic into a big pot. Add vegetable stock and milk and bring soup to a boil over medium heat. Cook for 10 minutes.
2. Puree the soup with a blender. Add salt, pepper, ginger and lemon juice.
3. Serve soup topped with fresh parsley.

Nutritional info (per serving): 324 calories; 12 g fat; 44.2 g carbohydrate; 12 g protein

Tofu Peanut Satay and Cucumber Skewerst

Cooking time: 10-15 minutes

Servings: 4

Ingredients:

- 1 block firm tofu, cubed
- 1 English cucumber, peeled into long thin ribbons
- 1 tablespoon peanut butter + 3 tablespoons
- 3 tablespoons tamari sauce + 2 teaspoons
- 2 tablespoons sesame oil
- 2 tablespoons maple syrup + 2 teaspoons
- 2 garlic cloves, minced
- ¼ cup coconut milk
- 1 tablespoon lime juice
- 1 teaspoon ginger, minced
- 1 pinch red pepper flakes
- 1 pinch sea salt
- ½ cup toasted peanuts, chopped
- 1 cup fresh mint leaves, chopped

Instructions:

1. Preheat the grill to medium high.
2. Mix 1 tablespoon peanut butter, 3 tablespoons tamari sauce, 2 tablespoons sesame oil, 2 tablespoons maple syrup and 1 garlic clove in a bowl. Add tofu cubes and toss well to coat. Let marinate for 10-15 minutes.
3. Cook the satay sauce. Mix coconut milk, 3 tablespoons peanut butter, 1 tablespoon lime juice, 2 teaspoons tamari sauce, 2 teaspoons maple syrup, ginger, 1 garlic clove, sea salt and pepper flakes in a bowl. Stir until smooth.
4. Thread the marinated tofu onto skewers. Place the skewers on the grill and cook for 3-4 minutes per side.
5. Mix cucumber slices with the cooked sauce in a bowl. Top the skewers with chopped peanuts, sauce (satay) drizzle and mint leaves. Serve with cucumbers.

Nutritional info (per serving): 239 calories; 20.6 g fat; 9.74 g carbohydrate; 8.3 g protein

Cauliflower Leek Casserole

Cooking time: 40 minutes

Servings: 4-6

Ingredients:

- ½ cauliflower head, cut into florets
- 3 cups leeks, chopped
- 1 cup raw cashews, soaked for at least 4 hours
- 2 garlic cloves

- 2 cups water
- 2/3 cup nutritional yeast
- ¼ teaspoon paprika
- ¼ teaspoon cayenne pepper
- Fresh parsley, chopped
- Salt, black pepper, to taste

Instructions:

1. Preheat the oven to 390F.
2. Steam cauliflower florets in a steamer for 5 -7 minutes until tender. Toss cauliflower and leeks together, transfer to a casserole dish.
3. Add cashews, garlic, water, nutritional yeast, salt and pepper to a food processor or a blender. Process until smooth.
4. Pour sauce on top of cauliflower and leeks until well covered. Bake for 40 minutes until sauce has thickened and leeks have softened and wilted.
5. Remove casserole dish from oven. Sprinkle with paprika, cayenne pepper and chopped fresh parsley.

Nutritional info (per serving): 352 calories; 25.9 g fat; 14 g carbohydrate; 15.4 g protein

Eggplant Steaks with Tomato Salad

Cooking time: 30 minutes
Servings: 4

Ingredients:

- 2 eggplants, thickly sliced
- ¼ cup balsamic vinegar + 1 tablespoon
- 1 tablespoon oil
- 6 roma tomatoes, chopped
- 2 garlic cloves, chopped
- ½ red onion, chopped
- ¼ cup parsley, chopped
- Salt, pepper, to taste

Instructions:

1. Season eggplant slices with salt and let rest for 30 minutes. Wash and pat dry.
2. Mix balsamic vinegar (1/4 cup), salt and pepper in a bowl. Add eggplant steaks and coat well with the mixture.
3. Preheat the oven to 400F. Cover the baking sheet with parchment paper and place steaks on the sheet. Bake steaks for 20 minutes.
4. Meanwhile, mix tomatoes, garlic, onion, parsley and 1 tablespoon vinegar in a bowl. Add oil and toss well to coat.
5. Serve steaks topped with tomato salad.

Nutritional info (per serving): 363 calories; 13 g fat; 53 g carbohydrate; 12 g protein

Cheesy Mexican Tortilla Bake

Cooking time: 25 minutes

Servings: 4-6

Ingredients:

- 1 cup raw unsalted cashews
- 1 cup salsa
- ¾ cup plain dairy-free yogurt
- ¼ cup water
- 1 ¼ teaspoons smoked paprika
- 1 ¼ teaspoons ground cumin
- 1 teaspoon fine sea salt
- 9 small corn tortillas, quartered
- 2 cans (15 oz) low-sodium black beans, drained and rinsed
- 2 cups frozen sweet corn
- Green onions, for serving

Instructions:

1. Preheat the oven to 350 F. Add cashews, yogurt, paprika, water, cumin and salt to a blender and process until smooth.
2. Place the salsa on the bottom of the baking dish, in one layer. Top with tortillas, beans, corn and cashew sauce. Repeat layers until all the ingredients are used.
3. Bake for 25 minutes. Serve topped with green onions.

Nutritional info (per serving): 239 calories; 20.6 g fat; 9.7 g carbohydrate; 8.3 g protein

Tomato Basil Soup

Cooking time: 5 minutes

Servings: 3

Ingredients:

- 7 cups canned tomatoes
- 3 cloves of garlic, minced
- 1 onion, chopped
- 1 cup basil
- ½ cup cashews
- 3 tablespoons nutritional yeast
- 1 tablespoon olive oil
- A pinch red pepper flakes
- Vegan cashew cream, for serving
- Salt, pepper, to taste

Instructions:

1. Preheat oil in a pan and add onion and garlic. Cook for 2-3 minutes.
2. Add tomatoes and basil, cook for 1 minute. Let cool a bit and transfer to a blender, process until smooth. Return to the pan.
3. Season with salt, pepper and red pepper flakes, cook for 3 minutes. Serve topped with cream.

Nutritional info (per serving): 198 calories; 9 g fat; 26 g carbohydrate; 5 g protein

Vegan Club Sandwich

Cooking time: 55 minutes

Servings: 2

Ingredients:

Sweet Potato Chips:
- 1 small sweet potato, thickly sliced
- 1 tablespoon mustard
- 1 tablespoon maple syrup
- Salt, black pepper, to taste

Miso Tahini Tofu:
- 4 oz. extra firm tofu
- ½ teaspoon miso paste
- 3 tablespoons tahini
- 1 teaspoon maple syrup
- 1 tablespoon water

For serving:
- 3 slices of bread, toasted
- ½ ripe avocado, sliced
- 1 kale leaf, washed, de-stemmed, and ripped into smaller pieces
- 1 roma tomato, thinly sliced

Instructions:

1. Preheat the oven to 375F. Arrange potato slices on the bottom of a baking dish in one layer.
2. Mix mustard, maple syrup, salt, and pepper in a bowl, and spread on top of potato chips. Bake for 20-30 minutes.
3. Pat dry tofu with paper towel. Mix miso paste, tahini, maply syrup and water in a bowl. Add tofu, toss well to coat and marinate for at least 10 minutes.
4. Place tofu on a baking tray in one layer and cook for 20-25 minutes.
5. Place avocado slices on top of each bread slice, top with kale and tomato, baked tofu and potato chips. Top with final piece of toast. Serve.

Nutritional info (per serving): 423 calories; 26.7 g fat; 38.9 g carbohydrate; 13.6 g protein

Creamy Red Pepper Alfredo Pasta

Cooking time: 10 minutes

Servings: 5

Ingredients:

- 1 red bell pepper, chopped
- ½ cup water
- ½ cup raw cashews
- ¼ cup nutritional yeast

- ¼ teaspoon onion powder
- ¼ teaspoon ground turmeric
- 1/8 teaspoon ground nutmeg
- 10 oz pasta of choice, cooked

Instructions:

1. Soak nuts in water for at least 6-8 hours. Drain and pat dry.
2. Add nuts, bell pepper, water, yeast, onion powder, ground turmeric and ground nutmeg to a blender and process until smooth.
3. Add sauce to a pan and preheat over medium heat. Cook for 1-2 minutes until hot.
4. Pour the sauce over pasta, toss well to coat and serve.

Nutritional info (per serving): 279 calories; 8.2 g fat; 41.2 g carbohydrate; 12.5 g protein

Sesame Noodles

Cooking time: 15 minutes

Servings: 4

Ingredients:

- 8 oz noodles of choice, uncooked
- 3 tablespoons rice vinegar
- 3 tablespoons coconut aminos
- 1 ½ tablespoons toasted sesame oil

- 2 tablespoons honey
- 1 tablespoon garlic, minced
- ¼ teaspoon ground ginger
- Sliced scallions, for serving
- Sesame seeds, for serving

Instructions:

1. Fill a medium sauce pan with water, add salt and bring to a boil. Add noodles and cook for 6-8 minutes. Drain the noodles.
2. Mix vinegar, sesame oil, coconut aminos, honey, garlic and ginger in a bowl.
3. Pour the sauce over pasta and toss well to coat. Serve topped with scallions and sesame seeds.

Nutritional info (per serving): 531 calories; 11.8 g fat; 60.2 g carbohydrate; 14.8 g protein

Vegan Pot Pie

Cooking time: 50 minutes

Servings: 4-6

Ingredients:

For the Dough:

- 2 cup flour

- ½ teaspoon baking powder
- ½ teaspoon salt
- ¼ cup canola oil
- ½ cup cold water

For the Filling:
- 1 lb meatless chicken breast, chopped
- 1 onion, diced
- 2 Yukon Gold potatoes, peeled and diced
- 2 carrots, diced
- 1 cup frozen peas
- 2 garlic cloves, minced
- 3 tablespoons canola oil
- 2 tablespoons fresh sage, chopped
- 2 teaspoons fresh thyme, chopped
- 3 tablespoons all-purpose flour
- 2 cups soy milk
- Salt, pepper, to taste

Instructions:

1. Cook the dough first: mix flour, baking powder and salt in a food processor.
2. Add oil and pulse until combined. Slowly add cold water through feed tube, pulsing constantly, until soft dough forms.
3. Form the dough into a ball, then flatten into disc. Wrap in a plastic wrap and chill for at least 30 minutes.
4. Preheat the oven to 375F. Heat oil in a sauce pan over medium heat.
5. Add onion and cook until softened for about 5 minutes. Add potatoes, carrots, garlic, sage, thyme, salt and pepper; cook for 2 minutes.
6. Add flour and cook for 1 minute more. Slowly stir in soy milk and ½ cup water, stirring constantly.
7. Add meatless chicken breasts and peas and bring everything to a boil. Reduce the heat to a simmer and cook for 2

minutes. Transfer the mixture to a glass baking dish. Cool slightly.

8. Roll out pie dough to rectangle, on lightly floured surface. Place over filling and pinching to form decorative border around edge. Cut 1 inch circular vent in centre.

9. Bake in centre of oven until golden brown on top, for about 40 minutes. Cool for 10 minutes before serving.

Nutritional info (per serving): 655 calories; 27.4 g fat; 88.1 g carbohydrate; 15.7 g protein

Vegan Spaghetti alla Puttanesca

Cooking time: 20 minutes

Servings: 4

Ingredients:

- 8 oz whole grain spaghetti
- 1 can (28 oz) chunky tomato sauce
- ⅓ cup Kalamata olives, chopped
- ⅓ cup capers
- 1 tablespoon Kalamata olive brine
- 1 tablespoon caper brine
- 3 garlic cloves, pressed or minced
- ¼ teaspoon red pepper flakes
- 1 tablespoon olive oil
- ½ cup fresh parsley leaves, chopped
- Salt, pepper, to taste

Instructions:

1. Mix tomato sauce, olives, capers, olive bring, caper brine, garlic and red pepper flakes in a bowl.
2. Add the mixture to a sauce pan and bring to a boil over medium heat. Reduce the heat to low and simmer for 20 minutes, stirring often.

3. Remove the sauce from heat, add olive oil and chopped parsley. Season with salt and pepper.
4. Bring a large pot of salted water to a boil and cook spaghetti according to package instructions. Drain.
5. Pour the sauce over pasta and stir to combine. Serve topped with more chopped parsley.

Nutritional info (per serving): 449 calories; 8.9 g fat; 84 g carbohydrate; 16.6 g protein

Grits with Tempeh Sausage and Brussels Sprouts

Cooking time: 25 minutes

Servings: 4

Ingredients:

- 8 oz tempeh, crumbled
- 1 onion, thinly sliced
- 8 oz Brussels sprouts, shredded
- 4 teaspoons vegetable oil
- 1 garlic clove, minced
- 1 teaspoon chili powder
- 1 teaspoon fennel seeds
- ¾ teaspoon smoked paprika
- ¾ cup low sodium vegetable broth
- 1 tablespoon tamari

- 2 teaspoons apple cider vinegar
- 1-2 teaspoons maple syrup (to taste)

For the Grits:
- 3 cups water
- 1 cup white corn grits
- 1 tablespoon olive oil
- 2 tablespoons nutritional yeast
- Salt, black pepper, to taste

Instructions:

1. Preheat 2 teaspoons of oil in a skillet over medium high heat. Add the tempeh and cook for 3-4 minutes, stirring frequently.
2. Add garlic and cook for 1 more minute, stirring constantly. Add chili, fennel, paprika, broth, tamari, vinegar, and maple syrup to the skillet. Bring everything to a boil and reduce the heat to low.
3. Cook until the broth has been absorbed. Transfer the crumbles to a plate and set aside.
4. Add 2 teaspoons oil to the same skillet. Add onion and Brussels sprouts, season with salt and pepper.
5. Cook for about 6-8 minutes, stirring occasionally. Add the sausage crumbles to onions and sprouts, mix well and adjust salt and pepper to taste. Remove from heat.
6. Bring water and salt to boil. Whisk in the grits and reduce the heat to medium low. Cook for 5-10 minutes, stirring constantly. Add vegan butter and nutritional yeast.
7. Serve grits with tempeh and sausage mixture on the side.

Nutritional info (per serving): 249 calories; 14.9 g fat; 18.6 g carbohydrate; 15.8 g protein

Minestrone Soup

Cooking time: 20 minutes

Servings: 6

Ingredients:

- 1 white onion, diced
- 3 garlic cloves, minced
- 3 carrots, chopped
- 2 celery ribs, chopped
- 1 can (28 oz) diced tomatoes with juices
- 4 cups vegetable broth
- 1 teaspoon dried basil
- 1 teaspoon dried oregano
- 1 ¼ cup pasta of choice, uncooked
- 1 can (19 oz) kidney beans, drained and rinsed
- Salt, pepper, to taste

Instructions:

1. Add 2-3 tablespoons of water or broth to a large sauce pan and add onions, garlic, carrots and celery. Cook over medium heat for 2-3 minutes, stirring frequently.
2. Add diced tomatoes, basil, oregano, broth, beans and pasta, simmer for about 10-15 minutes.
3. Season with salt and pepper and serve hot.

Nutritional info (per serving): 315 calories; 4.1 g fat; 53.8 g carbohydrate; 12.8 g protein

Mushrooms and Peas Vegan Risotto

Cooking time: 25 minutes

Servings: 4

Ingredients:

- 1 tablespoon olive oil
- 1 small onion, diced
- 2 garlic cloves, minced
- 1 ½ cup Arborio rice
- 4 cups vegetable broth
- ½ cup dry white wine
- ¾ cup frozen peas
- 2 tablespoons vegan butter
- Juice of one lemon
- 1 teaspoon lemon zest
- ½ teaspoon ground coriander
- 1 cup button mushrooms, sliced
- 1/3 cup vegan parmesan cheese, grated
- Salt, pepper, to taste

Instructions:

1. Add broth to a medium pan and heat it up over low heat for up to 10 minutes.

2. Heat oil in a large pan over medium heat. Add onion and garlic, cook for 4-5 minutes until onions are translucent. Add mushrooms, cook for 5 more minutes.
3. Add rice and cook for 1 more minute. Reduce heat to low.
4. Add white wine and lemon juice, Cook until almost all wine has dissolved, stir constantly.
5. Add 1 cup of vegetable broth to rice and cook until almost all broth evaporates. Add one more cup and repeat the process, until rice is soft and cooked. Add hot water to rice if you need more liquid.
6. Add peas, vegan butter, lemon zest, coriander, salt and pepper. Cook for 3-5 minutes.
7. Serve with vegan cheese on top.

Nutritional info (per serving): 386 calories; 5.4 g fat; 65.5 g carbohydrate; 12 g protein

Stewed Chickpeas and Chard Toast

Cooking time: 20 minutes

Servings: 4

Ingredients:

- 4 slices whole-wheat bread
- 1 can (14.5-oz.) diced tomatoes, unsalted
- 8 oz rainbow chard, chopped
- 6 garlic cloves, minced
- 3 tablespoons extra-virgin olive oil

- 1 cup yellow onion, chopped
- 1 teaspoon ground cumin
- ¾ teaspoon smoked paprika
- ¼ teaspoon crushed red pepper
- 1 can (15 oz) chickpeas, drained
- Salt, to taste

Instructions:

1. Preheat the broiler. Add tomatoes to a food processor and pulse until pureed.
2. Preheat 2 tablespoons oil in a skillet over medium heat. Add onion and garlic, cook for about 3 minutes.
3. Add chard and cook for 3 minutes, stirring occasionally. Add cumin, paprika, red pepper and salt, cook for about 30 seconds.
4. Add chickpeas and tomatoes and bring to a simmer. Reduce the heat to low and cover the skillet. Cook for about 5 minutes.
5. Place bread slices on a baking tray in one layer.
6. Cut remaining garlic clove in half. Place bread in a single layer on a baking sheet. Broil for about 1 minute. Turn bread over; brush with 1 tablespoon oil.
7. Top each slice with about 1 cup of chickpea mixture.

Nutritional info (per serving): 352 calories; 13 g fat; 48 g carbohydrate; 13 g protein

Broccoli Quinoa Gratin

Cooking time: 20 minutes

Servings: 4

Ingredients:

- 1 cup quinoa, rinsed
- 2 cups vegetable broth
- 1 cup soy or almond milk
- 1 can (15 oz) chickpeas
- 1 broccoli head, broken into florets
- 1 teaspoon onion powder
- 1 teaspoon ground oregano
- ¾ teaspoon paprika
- 1 tablespoon oil
- 3 tablespoons oats
- 1 tablespoon nutritional yeast flakes
- A pinch of turmeric
- 1 teaspoon soy sauce
- ½ teaspoon smoked paprika
- 7 oz vegan cheese sauce
- Salt, pepper, to taste

Instructions:

1. Preheat the oven to 400F.
2. Add vegetable broth to a sauce pan and bring to a boil. Add quinoa and simmer for 15-20 minutes.
3. Spread broccoli florets on a baking sheet in one layer, drizzle with little oil and season with salt. Bake for about 15 minutes.
4. Add oats, nutritional yeast, onion powder, 1 tablespoon oil, paprika, turmeric, soy sauce, salt and pepper to a bowl and mix well to combine.
5. Preheat oil in a sauce pan over medium heat, add breadcrumbs mixture, cook for about 30 seconds-1 minute.
6. Add 1 cup milk, remaining spices, chickpeas and half of the cheese sauce to quinoa and stir well.

7. Transfer the mixture into a lightly greased casserole dish, add broccoli florets and spread the rest of the cheese on top. Sprinkle with the "breadcrumbs".
8. Bake the casserole for about 10-15 minutes.

Nutritional info (per serving): 443 calories; 15.6 g fat; 47 g carbohydrate; 19 g protein

Vegan Spinach Artichoke Quesadillas

Cooking time: 8 minutes

Servings: 2-4

Ingredients:

- 2-4 flour tortillas
- 3 cups baby spinach
- 1 garlic clove, diced
- ½ teaspoon olive oil
- 6 oz marinated artichoke hearts, diced
- 4 oz vegan cream cheese
- 2 tablespoons vegan mayo
- Salt and pepper, to taste

Instructions:

1. Preheat olive oil in a pan over medium heat. Add garlic and cook for 1 minute, stirring frequently.
2. Add artichoke hearts and 2 cups of spinach. Stir well to combine and cook until spinach begins to wilt.

3. Add cream cheese, mayo, salt and pepper and stir to combine. Cook for 1 minute and set aside.
4. Preheat a big non stick pan over medium heat. Place 1 tortilla into the pan and fill with part of the spinach mixture. Add additional spinach on top. Fold tortilla in half and cook until bottom begins to brown, for about 2 minutes.
5. Flip and cook for 1 minute more. Repeat with the rest of tortillas.

Nutritional info (per serving): 128 calories; 9 g fat; 9.7 g carbohydrate; 2.6 g protein

Quinoa and Roasted Pepper Chili

Cooking time: 25 minutes

Servings: 4

Ingredients:

- 1/3 cup quinoa, uncooked, rinsed
- 1 can (14.5 oz) fire-roasted diced tomatoes with chipotles, undrained
- 1 can (15 oz) pinto beans, rinsed and drained
- 1 cup low-sodium vegetable broth
- 2 bell peppers, halved lengthwise, deseeded
- 2 poblano chiles, halved lengthwise, deseeded
- 4 teaspoons olive oil
- 3 cups zucchini, chopped
- 1 ½ cups onion, chopped

- 4 garlic cloves, minced
- 1 tablespoon chili powder
- 1 teaspoon ground cumin
- ½ teaspoon smoked paprika
- ½ cup water
- Salt, pepper, to taste

Instructions:

1. Preheat broiler.
2. Place bell pepper and chiles halves on a baking sheet lined with foil, skin sides up. Broil for 10 minutes. Place roasted peppers to a paper bag; close tightly. Let stand for 10 minutes. Peel and chop.
3. Preheat a large skillet over medium heat. Add oil, zucchini, onion and garlic, cook for 4 minutes.
4. Add chili powder, cumin and paprika, sauté for 30 seconds. Add peppers and chiles, water and remaining ingredients; bring to a boil.
5. Reduce heat to low, cover the pan and cook for 20 minutes.

Nutritional info (per serving): 258 calories; 6.3 g fat; 42.1 g carbohydrate; 9.7 g protein

Ratatouille

Cooking time: 20 minutes

Servings: 4

Ingredients:

- 1 onion, diced
- 2 bell peppers, better of different color, chopped
- 1 eggplant, cut into cubes
- 2 tomatoes, cut into large cubes
- 1 zucchini, sliced
- 4 garlic cloves, minced
- 1 tablespoon olive oil
- 1 bay leaf
- ½ cup tomato juice
- 5 tablespoons tomato paste
- 4 tablespoons dry red wine
- 1 teaspoon dried basil
- ½ teaspoon dried oregano
- ½ teaspoon dried rosemary
- ½ teaspoon dried marjoram
- Salt, pepper, to taste

Instructions:

1. Heat oil in a pan over medium heat. Add onion and sauté for 4-5 minutes until translucent.
2. Add red wine, bay leaf and tomato juice, mix well until combined.
3. Add basil, oregano, rosemary, marjoram, garlic, salt and pepper, stir well. Cover the pan and cook over low heat for 10 minutes.
4. Add zucchini and bell peppers, cook for 5 more minutes. Then add tomatoes, tomato paste and eggplant. Cover the pan and cook for 8-10 minutes.

5. Turn off the heat, stir the veggies and allow to cool a little before serving.

Nutritional info (per serving): 170 calories; 4 g fat; 31 g carbohydrate; 6 g protein

Vegan meatballs

Cooking time: 45 minutes

Servings: 12

Ingredients:

- 1 cup quinoa, cooked and cooled
- 1 can (15 oz) black beans, rinsed, drained and dried
- 2 tablespoons avocado oil
- 3 garlic cloves ,minced
- ½ cup shallot, diced
- 2 ½ teaspoons fresh oregano
- ½ teaspoon red pepper flakes
- ½ cup vegan parmesan cheese
- 2 tablespoons tomato paste
- 3 tablespoons fresh basil, chopped
- 2 tablespoons vegan Worcestershire sauce
- Salt, to taste

Instructions:

1. Preheat the oven to 350F.
2. Spread beans on a baking tray lined with parchment paper. Bake for 15 minutes. Remove from the oven and increase the temperature to 375F.
3. Preheat oil in a large skillet over medium heat. Add garlic and shallot, sauté for 2-3 minutes.
4. Add black beans, cooked garlic and shallots, oregano, red pepper flakes and salt to a food processor. Blend until loose. Add quinoa, vegan parmesan cheese, tomato paste, fresh basil and Worcestershire sauce. Pulse until combined.
5. Form the mixture into balls. Add to a plate and refrigerate for 15 minutes.
6. Preheat non stick skillet and add balls, sauté for couple of minutes until lightly brown on all sides. Transfer to a baking dish and bake for 20-30 minutes.

Nutritional info (per serving): 67.4 calories; 1.9 g fat; 10 g carbohydrate; 3.3 g protein

Creamed Spinach

Cooking time: 10 minutes

Servings: 2

Ingredients:

- 3 lbs fresh spinach, chopped
- ½ cup soy milk
- 1 ¼ cups water

- 1 package onion soup mix
- 1 teaspoon nutritional yeast

Instructions:

1. Add water to a medium sauce pan and bring to a boil. Add onion soup mix and stir well to combine, until dissolved.
2. Add spinach and reduce the heat to low. Cook for about 5 minutes, stirring occasionally.
3. Add soy milk and stir for a few minutes.
4. In a medium-sized saucepan, bring the water to a simmer and add the entire packet of onion soup or dip mix, stirring well to combine. Add nutritional yeast and stir well.
5. Remove from heat and serve.

Nutritional info (per serving): 83 calories; 6 g fat; 5 g carbohydrate; 3 g protein

Vegan Burrito

Cooking time: 10 minutes

Servings: 4-6

Ingredients:

- 4-5 large flour tortillas
- 1 can (15 oz) black beans, drained and rinsed
- 1 ½ cups white rice, cooked
- ½ cup corn kernels, canned

- ½ cup romaine lettuce, chopped
- 1 medium tomato, chopped
- 1 tablespoon extra virgin olive oil
- 1 teaspoon ground cumin
- 1 teaspoon dried oregano
- ¼ teaspoon garlic powder
- A pinch red pepper flakes
- 2 tablespoons fresh cilantro, chopped
- 1 avocado, mashed with a fork
- Salt, pepper, to taste

Instructions:

1. Preheat oil in a skillet, add beans, cumin, oregano, garlic powder, red pepper flakes, salt and pepper. Stir well and cook for 3-5 minutes.
2. Place tortilla on a work surface, stuff each tortilla with rice, beans, corn, lettuce, tomato, cilantro and avocado. Fold in the sides and roll up, then wrap in foil.
3. Cook the burritos in a skillet over medium heat for about 2-3 minutes on each side. Serve hot.

Nutritional info (per serving): 534 calories; 21.6 g fat; 75.1 g carbohydrate; 15.7 g protein

Tacos

Cooking time: 15 minutes

Servings: 12-16

Ingredients:

- 12-16 corn tortillas
- ½ onion, chopped
- 1 can (15 oz) black beans, drained
- 1 tablespoon olive oil
- 1 teaspoon crushed garlic
- ½ teaspoon ground cumin
- 2-3 cups salsa
- 1 cup tahini
- ¼ teaspoon cayenne pepper
- ¼ teaspoon chili flakes
- ½ teaspoon ground cumin
- 2–3 cups lettuce, shredded
- 2 avocados, peeled and chopped
- Salt, pepper, to taste

Instructions:

1. Preheat oil in a pan over medium heat, add onion, garlic, cayenne pepper, chili flakes and ground cumin, cook for 3-4 minutes.
2. Add black beans and cook for 1-2 minutes. Season with salt and pepper.
3. Stack the tortillas and cover with foil. Preheat in the oven at 350F for about 15 minutes.
4. Spread lettuce on each tortilla, top with beans, salsa, avocado and tahini sauce. Serve.

Nutritional info (per serving): 325 calories; 14.9 g fat; 42.2 g carbohydrate; 10.1 g protein

Pepperoni Pizza

Cooking time: 15 minutes

Servings: 2

Ingredients:

- 8 oz flour
- ½ cup water
- 1 tablespoon olive oil
- 2 teaspoons baking powder
- 2 tablespoons tomato paste
- 2 zucchini, thinly sliced
- ½ tomato, sliced
- ½ red onion, sliced
- ½ teaspoon hot sauce
- 2 tablespoons tamari
- 2 tablespoons balsamic vinegar
- Vegan cheese
- Salt, to taste

Instructions:

1. Mix hot sauce, tamari and vinegar in a bowl. Add zucchini and mix well to coat. Cover the bowl and marinate overnight in the fridge.
2. Mix flour, water, oil, baking powder and salt in a bowl, knead well. Let rest for 2-3 minutes.

3. Form the pizza crust, spread the dough on the working surface.
4. Preheat the oven to 390F.
5. Spread the tomato paste on top of the crust. Add marinated zucchini slices, tomato and onion. Top with vegan cheese.
6. Bake for 12-15 minutes.

Nutritional info (per serving): 536 calories; 8.69 g fat; 99.7 g carbohydrate; 16.7 g protein

Spinach Artichoke Pizza

Cooking time: 5 minutes

Servings: 12

Ingredients:

- 2 pre-made pizza dough
- 1 can artichoke hearts, drained, quartered
- 1 onion, chopped
- 5 cups fresh spinach
- 2 garlic cloves, minced
- 1 can white beans, rinsed and drained
- ¼ cup water
- 2 tablespoons nutritional yeast
- ½ cup cashews
- 1 tablespoon fresh lemon juice
- ½ cup vegan mozzarella cheese
- Salt, pepper, to taste

Instructions:

1. Preheat the oven to 350 F. Add beans, cashews, lemon juice, water and the yeast to a blender. Process until smooth.
2. Preheat oil in a pan and cook for about 3 minutes. Add garlic, 2 cups of spinach and cook for 3 minutes. Add processed white beans mixture, season with salt and pepper.
3. Spread the mixture on pizza dough, top with artichoke hearts and the remaining spinach. Sprinkle with cheese.
4. Bake for 8 minutes and serve.

Nutritional info (per serving): 177 calories; 6 g fat; 26 g carbohydrate; 7 g protein

Mushroom bean burger

Cooking time: 10 minutes

Servings: 5-6

Ingredients:

- ¾ cup mushrooms, diced
- 1 can (15 oz) pinto beans
- 3 tablespoons oil
- 1 onion, diced
- 1 garlic clove, minced
- 3 green onions, diced
- ½ teaspoon cumin
- 1 teaspoon parsley

- Salt, pepper, to taste

For Serving:
- Burger buns
- Sliced cucumber
- Tomato, sliced

Instructions:

1. Preheat 1 tablespoon oil in a skillet, add onion and garlic, cook for 3-5 minutes.
2. Add green onions, cumin and mushrooms and cook for 5 minutes.
3. Mash the beans with a fork, add onion mushroom mixture, parsley, salt and pepper. Mix well to combine.
4. Shape the mixture into patties. Heat 2 tablespoons oil in a skillet and cook patties for about 3 minutes on each side.
5. Serve patties on buns with cucumber and tomato.

Nutritional info (per serving): 313 calories; 4 g fat; 55 g carbohydrate; 18 g protein

Vegan Jambalaya

Cooking time: 30 minutes

Servings: 6-8

Ingredients:

- 1 cup rice, uncooked
- 3 cups water

- 1 cup canned chickpeas
- 1 cup canned kidney beans
- ½ onion, chopped
- 2 garlic cloves, chopped
- 1 bell pepper, chopped
- 1 carrot, chopped
- 1 can (14 oz) chopped tomatoes
- 2 tablespoons tamari sauce
- 2 teaspoons dried oregano
- 1 teaspoon dried thyme
- 1 teaspoon garlic powder
- 1 teaspoon onion powder
- 1 teaspoon cumin powder
- 1 teaspoon paprika
- 1/8 teaspoon cayenne powder
- Chopped fresh parsley, for serving
- Salt, pepper, to taste

Instructions:

1. Add all the vegetables to the sauce pan along with 3 tablespoons water. Cook for about 5 minutes.
2. Add tomatoes and cook for another 5 minutes. Add tamari and all the spices to the pan, stir well to combine.
3. Add rice and 3 cups water and bring to a boil. Cover and cook on medium high for 15 minutes.
4. Add tahini, chickpeas and beans, cook for 1-2 minutes. Serve with parsley on top.

Nutritional info (per serving): 305 calories; 4.1 g fat; 53.9 g carbohydrate; 13.8 g protein

Creamy Lemon Pepper Chickpeas

Cooking time: **15 minutes**
Servings: 4

Ingredients:

- 1 can (19 oz) chickpeas, drained and rinsed
- ¼ cup full fat coconut milk
- 1 tablespoon olive oil
- ½ onion, chopped
- 3 garlic cloves, minced
- 1 tablespoon flour
- 1 cup vegetable broth
- 1 lemon, zested
- 2 tablespoons lemon juice
- A handful cilantro, chopped
- Salt, pepper, to taste

Instructions:

1. Preheat oil in a skillet over medium heat. Add onions and garlic, cook for about 5 minutes.
2. Add flour and cook for 30 seconds more. Add broth, lemon juice, lemon zest, salt, and pepper. Deglaze the pan.
3. Add chickpeas and bring to a boil. Cook for 5-10 minutes.
4. Add coconut milk and stir well to combine. Serve topped with cilantro.

Nutritional info (per serving): 229 calories; 9.5 g fat; 30.1 g carbohydrate; 8.5 g protein

Potato Pancakes

Cooking time: 10 minutes

Servings: 10-12

Ingredients:

- 3 yukon gold potatoes, grated
- ½ yellow onion, grated
- ½ cup flour
- 2 green onions, chopped
- 2 garlic cloves, minced
- 1 Jalapeno, minced
- ¼ teaspoon baking powder
- 2-3 tablespoons oil
- Salt, pepper, to taste

Instructions:

1. Mix potatoes, onion, flour, green onions, garlic, Jalapeno, baking powder, salt and pepper in a bowl.
2. Add oil to a skillet and preheat over medium heat. Add about 1-2 tablespoons of potato mixture to the pan and form into patty. Cook for about 2 minutes per side. Repeat until all the mixture is used. Serve.

Nutritional info (per serving): 69 calories; 1 g fat; 12 g carbohydrate; 2 g protein

Tofu and Cauliflower Balti

Cooking time: 35 minutes

Servings: 4

Ingredients:

- 1 pack tofu, drained and pressed, cut into cubes
- 2 tablespoons oil
- 3 tablespoons flour
- ½ cauliflower head, cut into florets
- 1 cup vegetable stock
- ½ tablespoon garam masala
- 1 teaspoon coriander seeds
- 1 teaspoon cumin seeds
- 1 teaspoon mustard seeds
- 1 teaspoon fennel seeds
- 6 cardamon pods
- ¼ teaspoon cloves
- 2 bay leaves
- 1 teaspoon turmeric
- 2 tablespoons tomato puree
- 1 teaspoon ground ginger

- 2 garlic cloves
- 2 tablespoons coconut oil
- 1 – inch piece ginger, grated
- Salt, pepper, to taste

Instructions:

1. Dust tofu cubes in flour. Preheat 1 tablespoon oil in a skillet and cook tofu for 5 minutes.
2. Add coriander seeds, cumin seeds, mustard seeds, fennel seeds, cardamom pods and bay leaves to a non stick frying pan. Dry fry for 1-2 minutes. Transfer to a blender and process until smooth.
3. Mix the processed spices, turmeric, curry powder, ground ginger, puree, vinegar, coconut oil, garlic and ginger in a bowl. Stir into a paste.
4. Add about 1 tablespoon oil to a pan, heat over medium heat. Add tofu and cauliflower, cook for 3 minutes. Add stock, salt and pepper and cook for 10 minutes.
5. Add garam masala and fresh coriander, stir, cooking for 3 minutes. Serve over rice.

Nutritional info (per serving): 183 calories; 15.2 g fat; 9.6 g carbohydrate; 4 g protein

Coconut Apple Ginger Dal

Cooking time: 20 minutes

Servings: 4

Ingredients:

- 1 piece (3-inch) ginger, peeled, chopped
- 1 apple, grated
- 1 ½ cups lentils
- 1 can (13.5 oz) coconut milk
- ½ onion, chopped
- 2 garlic cloves, chopped
- 2 tablespoons virgin coconut oil
- ¼ teaspoon cayenne pepper
- ¼ teaspoon ground cumin
- ¼ teaspoon ground turmeric
- 2 tablespoons fresh lime juice
- 2 ½ cups water
- Salt, pepper, to taste

Instructions:

1. Preheat oil in a pot over medium heat. Add cayenne, cumin and turmeric, cook for about 1 minute, stirring.
2. Add onion, garlic and ginger, cook for 3 minutes. Add apple and lentils and stir to combine everything.
3. Add coconut milk and water, bring everything to a boil. Reduce the heat to low and cook for 20-25 minutes, stirring occasionally.
4. Season with salt and pepper and add lime juice. Serve.

Nutritional info (per serving): 430 calories; 15.2 g fat; 56.3 g carbohydrate; 20.4 g protein

Vegetable Risotto

Cooking time: **25 minutes**

Servings: **4**

Ingredients:

- 3.5-4 cups vegetable broth
- 2 tablespoons water (or oil), divided
- 1 small bundle asparagus, ends trimmed (or 1 small bundle broccolini, stalks trimmed (or use both)
- 1 medium red bell pepper, seeds and stems removed, thinly sliced
- 1/4 teaspoon sea salt
- 1/4 teaspoon black pepper
- 3/4 cup thinly sliced shallot
- 1 cup arborio rice
- 1/4 cup dry white wine (or sub more vegetable broth)
- 1/4 cup vegan parmesan cheese (plus more for serving)
- fresh chopped parsley, for serving (optional)

Instructions:

1. Put vegetable broth into a medium saucepan and heat it on a medium heat. Then once simmering, reduce the heat to low to keep warm.

2. Preheat a large pan on a medium heat, and once hot, add half of water (or oil), asparagus (and/or broccolini) and red bell pepper. Then season with a pinch of salt and pepper.
3. Sauté for 3-4 minutes stirring frequently until just tender and slightly browned. Then cover to steam and speed the cooking time, and remove from the pan, uncover, and set aside.
4. Preheat another large rimmed pan on a medium heat, and once hot, add the remaining water (or oil), shallot and sauté for 1-2 minutes or until softened and very slightly browned.
5. Add arborio rice and cook for 1 minute, stirring occasionally. Then add dry white wine (or more vegetable broth) and stir gently, cook for 1-2 minutes or until the liquid is absorbed.
6. By using a ladle, add warmed vegetable broth 1/2 cup at a time, stirring almost constantly, giving the risotto little breaks to come back to a simmer (the heat should be medium, and there should always be a slight simmer, and you want the mixture to be cooking but not boiling or it will get gummy and cook too fast).
7. Continue to add vegetable broth 1 ladle at a time, stirring to incorporate, until the rice is cooked through, but not mushy (the whole process should only take 15-20 minutes and may take longer if making a larger batch).
8. Once the rice is cooked through, remove it from heat and season with salt and pepper to taste. Also add vegan parmesan cheese and most of the cooked vegetables, reserving a few for serving. Stir to coat.
9. Taste and adjust flavor as needed, adding a pinch of salt and pepper to taste or more vegan parmesan to enhance the cheesiness.

Nutritional info (per serving): 257 calories; 2.2 g fat; 50 g carbohydrate; 5.7 g protein

Coconut Curry Ramen

Cooking time: 1 hour 15 minutes

Servings: 4

Ingredients:

- 2 tablespoons toasted or untoasted sesame oil
- 2 small knobs ginger, sliced lengthwise into long strips
- 10 cloves garlic, chopped
- 2 large onions, chopped lengthwise
- 5 tablespoons yellow or green curry paste
- 8 cups vegetable broth
- 4 cups light coconut milk
- 2-4 tablespoons coconut sugar (optional)
- 1 teaspoon ground turmeric (optional)
- 2 tablespoons white or yellow miso paste
- 4-6 cups noodles of choice
- fresh green onion, chopped (optional)
- sriracha or chili garlic sauce (optional)

Instructions:

1. Preheat a large pot on a medium-high heat, and once hot, add oil, garlic, ginger, onion.
2. Sauté stirring occasionally for 5-8 minutes or until the onion has browned edges.

3. Then add curry paste and sauté for 1-2 minutes more, stirring frequently.
4. Add vegetable broth and coconut milk and stir to deglaze the bottom of the pan.
5. Bring to a simmer on a medium heat, reduce the heat to low and cover. Simmer on low for at least 1 hour, stirring occasionally (the longer it cooks, the more the flavor will deepen and develop).
6. Taste broth and adjust the seasonings as needed, adding coconut sugar for a little sweetness, turmeric for more intense curry flavor, or more sesame oil for nuttiness.
7. About 10 minutes before serving, prepare any desired toppings/sides, such as noodles, or green onion (optional).
8. Just before serving, scoop out 1/2 cup of the broth and whisk in the miso paste. Once fully dissolved, add back to the pot and turn off the heat and stir to combine.
9. Either strain broth through a fine mesh strainer (discard onions and ginger or add back to the soup) or ladle out the broth and leave the onions and mushrooms behind.
10. To serve, divide noodles of choice between the serving bowls. Top with broth and desired toppings. Serve with chili garlic sauce or sriracha sauce.

Nutritional info (per serving): 417 calories; 19.4 g fat; 56 g carbohydrate; 8.9 g protein

Sweet Potato Noodle Pasta

Cooking time: **10 minutes**

Servings: 4

Ingredients:

For the sauce:

- 1 cup raw cashews
- 3 cloves garlic (add more or less to taste for preferred garlicky flavor)
- 4-5 tablespoons nutritional yeast
- 1/2 teaspoon sea salt
- 2 teaspoon arrowroot starch (or cornstarch; for thickening)
- 1.5-2 cups unsweetened plain almond or rice milk (more as needed)
- 1 pinch red pepper flake (optional)

For noodles:

- 3 medium sweet potatoes, peeled and spiralized
- fresh parsley, chopped (for serving, optional)
- sautéed kale or kale chips (for serving, optional)
- crispy chickpeas (for serving, optional)

- vegan parmesan cheese (for serving, optional)
- red pepper flakes (for serving, optional)

Instructions:

1. Put cashews into a small mixing bowl and soak for 30 minutes in a very hot water. Then drain thoroughly and set aside. (Or soak cashews overnight or 6-8 hours in cool water).
2. If serving with kale chips or sautéed kale (or crispy chickpeas), prepare now and set aside until serving.
3. Once cashews are ready, peel and spiralize potatoes. Set aside.
4. Put drained cashews, garlic, nutritional yeast, salt, arrowroot starch, and almond or rice milk into a high-speed blender.
5. Blend on high until creamy and smooth, scraping the sides as needed. Taste and adjust the flavor. If too thick, thin with a bit more almond milk.
6. Put sauce into a large, rimmed pan or pot and heat on a medium-low heat constantly whisling until it starts bubbling. Once bubbling, reduce the heat to a very low simmer to keep warm. If too thick, thin with a bit more almond milk.
7. Pour 1 inch water to a large pot, put a steamer basket on top and heat on a medium-high heat until it starts bubbling. Once bubbling, add potato noodles, cover to steam for 3-5 minutes or until cooked or soften a bit (depending on taste).
8. Add sweet potatoes to the sauce and gently toss to combine. If using kale or other add-ins, this the time to add.
9. Serve as is or garnish with fresh parsley, crispy chickpeas, kale, vegan parmesan, or red pepper flake (optional).

Nutritional info (per serving): 417 calories; 19.4 g fat; 56 g carbohydrate; 8.9 g protein

Vegan Poutine

Cooking time: **45 minutes**

Servings: 6

Ingredients:

For the fries:

- 4 medium russet potatoes, unpeeled (or sub sweet potatoes for a savory-sweet poutine)
- 3-4 tablespoons avocado or melted coconut oil
- 1/2 teaspoon sea salt

For the gravy:

- 3 tablespoons avocado or melted coconut oil
- 2 medium shallots (minced)
- 1 1/2 cups diced button or cremini mushrooms
- 1/4 teaspoon each sea salt and black pepper (plus more to taste)
- 1 tablespoon balsamic vinegar
- 1 teaspoon coconut aminos (optional)
- 3 tablespoons cornstarch (or arrowroot)
- 1/2 cup vegetable broth
- 1 cup unsweetened plain almond milk
- 1-2 teaspoon vegan Worcestershire sauce or ketchup (optional)

- 1 batch vegan mozzarella cheese", separated into 1 teaspoon amounts

Instructions:

1. Chop potatoes into thin slices by halving lengthwise and cutting into wedges and strips. For wedges, cut into larger pieces.
2. Line two large baking sheets with parchment paper, then put fries, oil, salt and toss to coat. Arrange fries in a single layer, making sure they aren't overlapping too much.
3. Preheat the oven to 450F and bake for a total of 25-35 minutes, tossing/flipping at least once to ensure even baking. Once cooked, remove from oven and set aside.
4. Prepare the gravy by heating a rimmed skillet on a medium heat. Once hot, add oil (or water), shallots and sauté for 2-3 minutes, stirring occasionally.
5. Then add mushrooms, salt, pepper, balsamic vinegar, and coconut aminos (optional). Stir.
6. Increase the heat to a medium high to brown mushrooms, cook for 4-5 minutes or until slightly caramelized. Add cornstarch and stir to coat.
7. Lower the heat to low and slowly add broth and almond milk while whisking. Cook for 4-5 minutes, or until you've reached the desired consistency. If too thick, thin with a bit more almond milk.
8. Put into a blender and blend until smooth. Taste and adjust the flavor as needed
9. Return gravy to stovetop and heat on a lowest heat to keep warm.

Nutritional info (per serving): 432 calories; 28.4 g fat; 40.3 g carbohydrate; 7.5 g protein

Cauliflower Rice Kitchari

Cooking time: **45 minutes**

Servings: 4

Ingredients:

- 3/4 cup moong dal or chana dal
- 1.5 tablespoons coconut or avocado oil
- 1.5 teaspoon cumin seed
- 1 teaspoon mustard seed
- 2 tablespoons grated (or finely chopped) ginger
- 1-2 small serrano peppers, seeds removed, diced
- 1/4 teaspoon asafoetida
- 1 cup diced tomatoes
- 2 cups water
- 2 whole cloves (optional)
- 2 whole cardamom pods (optional)
- 2 cups cauliflower rice
- 1/2 teaspoon garam masala
- 1 teaspoon ground cumin
- 1 teaspoon ground turmeric (plus more to taste)
- 2-3 tablespoons coconut aminos (plus more to taste)
- 1/4 teaspoon sea salt (plus more to taste)
- 1/3 cup light coconut milk (optional)

Instructions:

1. Put moong dal (or chana dal) into a large pot or a skillet, top with cold water and soak overnight (or for 6 hours). Once soaked, rinse, drain and set aside in strainer.
2. Heat the same large pot or rimmed skillet on a medium heat, and once hot, add oil (or water), cumin seed, mustard seed, ginger, serrano peppers, asafoetida, and tomatoes. Sauté for a few minutes, stirring occasionally.
3. Next, add moong dal and sauté for a few minutes, stirring occasionally. Then add water, clove (optional), and cardamom (optional). Increase the heat and bring to a low boil.
4. Then reduce the heat to a simmer, cover, and cook for about 15-20 minutes until moong dal is tender.
5. Add cauliflower rice, garam masala, cumin, turmeric, coconut aminos, sea salt and stir to combine. Cover and cook for about 10-15 minutes stirring occasionally until cauliflower rice is tender. If the mixture becomes too dry, add more water.
6. Add coconut milk at this time for creamier texture (optional). Taste and adjust the flavor as needed.
7. Serve as is or over rice, greens, or roasted vegetables.

Nutritional info (per serving): 270 calories; 5.7 g fat; 40 g carbohydrate; 15.7 g protein

Moroccan-Spiced Eggplant and Tomato Stew

Cooking time: **50 minutes**

Servings: 4

Ingredients:

- 1 large eggplant (7 cups), unpeeled and cut into bite-size pieces
- 2 tablespoons olive or melted coconut oil
- 1/2 teaspoon sea salt
- 2 tablespoons olive or coconut oil
- 1 large white or yellow onion, thinly sliced
- 3 cloves garlic, minced
- 1 tablespoon ground cumin
- 1 tablespoon smoked paprika
- 1/4 teaspoon sea salt (plus more to taste)
- 2 cans (14.5-oz) diced fire-roasted tomatoes
- 1/2 cup water (or vegetable broth)
- 1 cup cooked chickpeas, well rinsed and drained (optional)
- 1 tablespoon maple syrup or coconut sugar
- 2 tablespoons harissa paste
- cilantro or parsley
- white rice, brown rice, or quinoa (or sub cauliflower rice* for grain-free)

- fresh lemon

Instructions:

1. Preheat the oven to 425F and line a large baking sheet with parchment paper.
2. Put diced eggplant, drizzle with avocado or olive oil, sprinkle with salt and toss to coat and roast for 30-35 minutes, flipping/tossing near the 20-minute mark.
3. Heat a large rimmed pan or pot on a medium heat, and once hot, add oil (or water) and onions. Sauté for 4-5 minutes, stirring frequently, or until soft and slightly caramelized.
4. Add garlic, cumin, paprika and stir to coat. Cook for 1 more minute.
5. Add tomatoes and their juices as well as water (or vegetable broth). Cover and bring to a simmer on a medium heat, and cook for 4 minutes to allow flavors to develop.
6. Remove the cover and add rinsed and drained chickpeas (optional), maple syrup, harissa paste and stir to coat. Then cover and simmer on a medium-low heat.
7. Remove the roasted eggplant from the oven, turn the oven off, and add eggplant to the tomatoes and chickpeas. Stir to combine and cover. Simmer on a medium-low/low heat for another 10 minutes to allow flavors to deepen.
8. Taste and adjust the flavors as needed.
9. Serve as is or over rice or grain of choice (or pasta or roasted vegetables) with wedges of fresh lemon and fresh chopped parsley or cilantro.

Nutritional info (per serving): 240 calories; 14.1 g fat; 25.7 g carbohydrate; 2.2 g protein

Red Curry with Roasted Vegetables

Cooking time: **25 minutes**

Servings: 4

Ingredients:

- 1 large sweet potato, cubed, skin on
- 2 cups broccoli or cauliflower, chopped, large stems removed
- 1 1/2 cups red cabbage, sliced
- 1 tablespoon neutral oil, divided
- 1 tablespoon maple syrup
- 1 teaspoon curry powder
- 1/4 teaspoon sea salt
- 2 tablespoons coconut oil
- 2/3 cup shallot, chopped
- 6 cloves garlic, minced
- 5 tablespoons ginger, freshly minced
- 6 tablespoons red curry paste
- 2 cans (14-oz) light coconut milk
- 1 healthy pinch sea salt (plus more to taste)
- 1/2 teaspoon ground turmeric
- 2 tablespoons maple syrup
- 2 tablespoons coconut aminos (or sub tamari or soy sauce if not gluten-free)

- 2 tablespoons lime juice (plus more to taste)
- cauliflower rice, quinoa, or rice
- cilantro
- lime wedges

Instructions:

1. Preheat the oven to 375F and line a baking sheet (or more, as needed) with parchment paper.
2. Put vegetables, oil, maple syrup, curry powder, sea salt into a mixing bowl and toss.
3. Put sweet potatoes into a baking sheet (leaving broccoli and cabbage behind) and roast for 10 minutes. At the 10-minute mark, remove pan from the oven, add broccoli and cabbage and return to the oven and roast for 12-15 more minutes.
4. Prepare curry by heating a large rimmed skillet or pot on a medium heat, and once hot, add coconut oil (or water), shallot, garlic, ginger and sauté for 3 minutes, stirring frequently.
5. Add curry paste and cook for 2 minutes, stirring occasionally.
6. Then add coconut milk, sea salt, turmeric, maple syrup, coconut aminos, whisk to combine, and once bubbling, reduce the heat to low and simmer for 10 minutes more minutes.
7. Add lime juice, taste and adjust the flavors as needed.
8. To serve, divide the sauce between serving bowls and rest some veggies in the center along with a spoonful of (optional) rice or grain of choice. Garnish with cilantro or lime wedges (optional).

Nutritional info (per serving): 417 calories; 22.8 g fat; 45.5 g carbohydrate; 8 g protein

Vegan Pizza

Cooking time: **20 minutes**

Servings: 2

Ingredients:

- 1/2 of garlic-herb pizza crust
- 1/2 cup each red, green, and orange bell pepper, loosely chopped
- 1/3 cup red onion, chopped
- 1 cup button mushrooms, chopped
- 1/2 teaspoon each dried or fresh basil, oregano, and garlic powder
- 1/4 teaspoon sea salt
- 1 can (15-oz) tomato sauce
- 1/2 teaspoon each dried or fresh basil, oregano, garlic powder, granulated sugar
- 1/4 teaspoon sea salt
- 1/2 cup vegan parmesan cheese
- red pepper flakes
- dried oregano

Instructions:

1. Put a rack into the middle of the oven.
2. Heat a large skillet on a medium heat, and once hot add 1 tablespoon olive oil, onion and peppers. Season with salt, herbs and stir, and cook for 10-15 minutes until soft and

slightly charred adding the mushrooms in the last few minutes. Once cooked, set aside.

3. Make sauce by putting tomato sauce into a mixing bowl, adding seasonings and salt to taste. Set aside.

4. Roll out the dough onto a floured surface and transfer to a parchment-lined round baking sheet. Put pizza with the parchment directly into the oven to properly crisp the crust, so any round object will do as it's not actually going into the oven.

5. Top with the desired amount of tomato sauce, a sprinkle of parmesan cheese and the sautéed veggies.

6. Use the baking sheet to gently slide the pizza directly onto the oven rack with the parchment underneath. Otherwise it will fall through.

7. Preheat the oven to 425F and bake for 17-20 minutes or until crisp and golden brown.

8. Serve with the remaining parmesan cheese, dried oregano and red pepper flake.

Nutritional info (per serving): 395 calories; 13 g fat; 59 g carbohydrate; 15 g protein

Vegan Thai Curry

Cooking time: **40 minutes**

Servings: 3

Ingredients:

- 2 lemongrass stalks, tough outer leaves removed, core finely chopped
- 5 spring onions, chopped
- handful fresh coriander, chopped
- 8 dried kaffir lime leaves
- 2 tablespoons tamari
- 2 green chillies, deseeded
- thumb-sized piece ginger, chopped

For the curry:

- 2 aubergines, roughly chopped
- 1 red pepper, roughly chopped
- 2 tablespoons coconut oil, melted
- 1 tablespoon sesame oil
- 1.66 cup green beans, cut into thirds
- 1.26 cup vegetable stock
- 13.5 oz can coconut milk (cream only)
- 10.6 oz buckwheat noodles
- handful cashew nuts
- 4 tablespoons desiccated coconut

Instructions:

1. Heat the oven to 395F. To make curry, put aubergines, red pepper, 1 tablespoon coconut oil in a roasting tin with, and roast for 20-25 mins until they are softened.
2. To make the paste put all the ingredients into a food processor and blend until smooth.
3. Heat sesame oil and the remaining coconut oil in a frying pan or wok, then add paste and fry for 1-2 minutes, then stir in green beans and fry for another 1-2 minutes.
4. Add vegetable stock, mixing well, followed by the roasted vegetables and the solid coconut cream from the top of the can of coconut milk. Give it all a good stir, bring to the boil, then allow it to simmer for 4-5 minutes.
5. Cook the buckwheat noodles following pack instructions.

6. Add cashews and desiccated coconut to the curry. Divide drained noodles between three bowls, top with curry, squeeze over some lime juice and garnish with red chilli.

Nutritional info (per serving): 654 calories; 36 g fat; 78 g carbohydrate; 12 g protein

Lentil Lasagna

Cooking time: 1 hour 15 minutes

Servings: 4

Ingredients:

- 1 tablespoon olive oil
- 1 onion, chopped
- 1 carrot, chopped
- 1 celery stick, chopped
- 1 garlic clove, crushed
- 2 cans (13.5 oz) lentils, drained, rinsed
- 1 tablespoon cornflour
- 13.5 oz can chopped tomato
- 1 teaspoon mushroom ketchup
- 1 teaspoon chopped oregano (or 1 teaspoon dried)
- 1 teaspoon vegetable stock powder
- 2 cauliflower heads, broken into florets
- 2 tablespoons unsweetened soy milk
- pinch of freshly grated nutmeg

- 9 dried egg-free lasagne sheets
- Vegan cheese

Instructions:

1. Heat oil in a pan, add onion, carrot, celery, and gently cook for 10-15 minutes until soft.
2. Add garlic, cook for a few more minutes, then stir in the lentils and corn flour.
3. Add tomatoes, a canful of water, mushroom ketchup, oregano, stock powder, some seasoning and simmer for 15 minutes, stirring occasionally.
4. Cook cauliflower in a pan of boiling water for 10 minutes or until tender. Once cooked, drain, purée with the soy milk using a hand blender or a food processor. Season well and add nutmeg.
5. Heat the oven to 356F. Spread a third of the lentil mixture over the base of a ceramic baking dish, about 8 x 12 inch. Cover with a single layer of lasagne, snapping the sheets to fit. Add another third of the lentil mixture, then spread a third of the cauliflower purée on top, followed by a layer of pasta. Top with the last third of lentils and lasagna, followed by the remaining purée.
6. Cover loosely with foil and bake for 35-45 minutes, removing the foil for the final 10 minutes of cooking. Serve topped with vegan cheese.

Nutritional info (per serving): 340 calories; 8.5 g fat; 47.1 g carbohydrate; 19.6 g protein

Mushroom Stroganoff

Cooking time: **25 minutes**

Servings: 4

Ingredients:

- 2 tablespoons olive oil
- 1/2 yellow onion, diced
- 2 garlic cloves, finely chopped
- 1 lb baby portobello mushrooms, sliced
- 1.5 cups vegetable broth
- 2 teaspoons soy sauce or tamari
- 1 teaspoon dried thyme
- 1/2 cup vegan sour cream
- 2 tablespoons whole wheat flour
- 1 lb farfalle pasta, cooked
- salt and black pepper, to taste
- fresh parsley, chopped

Instructions:

1. Heat olive oil in a pan on a medium heat. Add onion, garlic and cook for about 5 minutes until fragrant and the onion is soft.
2. Add mushrooms and cook for about 7 minutes until juices are released and become soft.

3. Add vegetable broth, soy sauce or tamari, thyme, and stir to combine. Reduce the heat to a medium-low and simmer for about 10 minutes until the liquid has reduced by a third.
4. Add vegan sour cream, flour and continue to simmer for another 3 minutes until the sauce thickens. Once done, remove from the heat.
5. Cook pasta according to package directions, until ready. Then drain, rinse and return noodles to the pot.
6. Pour the mushroom sauce over pasta and stir to coat. Season with salt and black pepper to taste.
7. Garnish with freshly chopped parsley and serve immediately.

Nutritional info (per serving): 345 calories; 6 g fat; 60 g carbohydrate; 13 g protein

9 781990 169595